Cover:
The Canal du Midi in Toulouse.

From left to right:
Argeliers Bridge (Aude).
Saint-Nazaire Cathedral and the old town of Béziers seen from the banks of the River Orb (Hérault).

ROUTES OF DISCOVERY

The Canal du Midi and navigable waterways

from the Atlantic to the Mediterranean

TEXT **René Gast**
PHOTOGRAPHS **Bruno Barbier**
TRANSLATION **Dédicace**

Editions OUEST-FRANCE

BORDEAUX
TOULOUSE
Garonne navigable
Lot navigable
Canal latéral à la Garonne
Canal latéral à la Garonne
Baïse navigable
Canal du Midi
Castets-en-Dorthe
Buzet-sur-Baïse
Villeneuve-sur-Lot
Valence-sur-Baïse
Luzech
Cahors
St-Cirq-Lapopie
Seuil de Naurouze
GIRONDE 33
LANDES 40
LOT-ET-GARONNE 47
DORDOGNE 24
CORRÈZE 19
LOT 46
TARN-ET-GARONNE 82
GERS 32
TARN 81
HAUTE-GARONNE 31
PYRÉNÉES-ATLANTIQUES 64
HAUTES-PYRÉNÉES 65
ARIÈGE 09
Lesparre-Médoc
Blaye
Libourne
Périgueux
Bergerac
Sarlat-la-Canédat
Brive-la-Gaillarde
Tulle
Gourdon
Figeac
Villefranche-de-Rouergue
Langon
Bazas
Marmande
Agen
Nérac
Condom
Mont-de-Marsan
Aire-sur-l'Adour
Auch
Mirande
Castelsarrasin
Montauban
Albi
Castres
Muret
Villefranche-de-Lauragais
Castelnaudary
Orthez
Pau
Tarbes
Oloron-Ste-Marie
Bagnères-de-Bigorre
Argelès-Gazost
St-Gaudens
St-Girons
Pamiers
Foix
Limoux
Col d'Aubisque 1709
2115 Col du Tourmalet
Col d'Aspin 1489
Col des Ares 796
Col du Portet d'Aspet 1069
Gironde
Dronne
Isle
Dordogne
Vézère
Corrèze
Garonne
Lot
Baïse
Gers
Aveyron
Viaur
Tarn
Agout
Save
Ariège
Aude
Douze
Midouze
Midou
Adour
Gave de Pau
Gave d'Oloron
Gave d'Aspe
Gave d'Ossau
A 10
A 89
A 20
A 63
A 66
A 62
A 61
A 64
A 68
A 680
N 10
N 124
N 20

Summary

AVEYRON
GARD 30
HÉRAULT 34
AUDE 11
Viaur
Tarn
Millau
A 75
Le Vigan
Gardon d'Alès
Gardon
Alès
Gard (ou Gardon)
A 9
Hérault
Nîmes
Beaucaire
Lodève
Montpellier
Arles
A 54
Étang de Mauguio
Agout
Orb
Étang de Vic
Petit Rhône
Grand Rhône
Étang de Vaccarès
Canal du Midi
Canal du Rhône à Sète
Béziers
Sète
Étang de Thau
Agde
Trèbes
Aude
Canal de Jonction
Carcassonne
A 61
Narbonne
Canal de la Robine
Étang de Bages et de Sigean
Étang de l'Ayrolles
Port-la-Nouvelle
GOLFE
DU LION
0
40 km

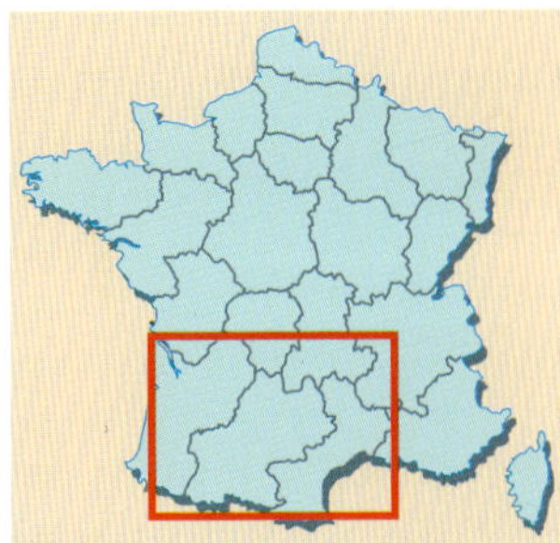

Introduction

Portrait of Riquet. Toulouse, Paul-Dupuy Museum.
Inv. No. D.61.6.29. Photo STC.

Our modern world, obsessed with speed and deafened by noise, very nearly condemned them to the black hole of history. Forgotten canals, abandoned rivers... only very recently, these water routes were anachronisms from a time when slowness was a way of life and silence was a virtue. But, fortunately, there are people with desires for discovery other than those satisfied by motorways, airplanes and TGV high-speed trains. There is only true "otherness" for those who know how to take time to look, devote time to emotion and give time for time. This is what, from lock to lock, the peace of the "routes of silence" offers. A growing number have understood this and they help give back life to the canals and rivers. This may be where true "modernity" lies – in finding a compromise with a different pace of life, with a forgotten past where journeys were calculated not in terms of the number of kilometres but the number of days, weeks or months...

36 Toulouse
Les Ecluses des Minimes

History of a masterpiece

Augustus, Nero, Charlemagne, François I, Henri IV, Louis XIII... They all had the same dream but none of them was able to come up with even the slightest outline of the project. From Antiquity to the modern era, the idea of joining the Mediterranean to the Atlantic via a "water route" made up of a canal and navigable rivers – or rivers made navigable – was governed by reason, but prevented by technical and financial realities for many long years.

After all, was it not only normal, on the one hand, to want to offer ships the opportunity to avoid the long and dangerous route around the Iberian peninsula – almost 3,000 kilometres – in seas overrun by Barbary pirates, some parts of which, for example the Gulf of

Left page:
Statue of Paul Riquet in Toulouse.

Engraving of Carcassonne (end of the 19th century).

The Canal du Midi at the Seuil de Naurouze, the highest point between the Atlantic and the Mediterranean.

The Canal du Midi at Boulevard de Monplaisir in Toulouse.

Gascony, were among the most dangerous in the world? And, on the other hand, to want to escape from the constraints of travel overland – slow, difficult, subject to attacks by bandits and only suitable for light loads – and prefer transport by waterway, faster and safer, cheaper and, above all, more efficient because a horse towing a boat was able to pull twenty times its weight compared to two times its weight when harnessed to a land-based vehicle?

But, how to channel the rivers flowing down from the Pyrenees and the Massif Central, more often than not mountain streams subject to devastating spates? How could the watershed at an altitude of 190 metres be crossed? How to provide a regular supply of water to a canal passing through regions often affected by long periods of drought? More than the cost of such a construction, it was the technical difficulties and particularly the canal's water supply which, for almost two thousand years, presented an obstacle to the dreams of some of the most powerful monarchs in the world.

At the start of the reign of Louis XIV, the problem of the Atlantic-Mediterranean junction became a major concern. Adopting part of the policy introduced by Richelieu, Colbert wanted to make France a centralised country which required the reinforcement of its means of communication, therefore implying the construction of ports, roads and canals. Shortening distances and reducing travel time meant bringing closer together, temporally and spatially, the main agri-

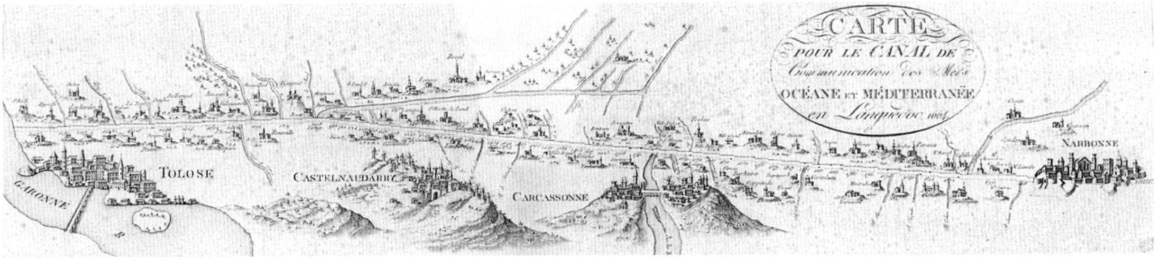

Map of the canal for Communication between the Ocean and Mediterranean Sea in Languedoc, 1664
Toulouse, Paul-Dupuy Museum
Inv. No. 711. Photo STC.

cultural and manufacturing areas – which included Languedoc and Aquitaine – and, thus, both supporting their growth and strengthening royal power in remote and, often, recalcitrant provinces. To these economic and political motives were added ulterior motives of strategy: developing maritime and overland transport routes would help give France a central role in Europe and combat the power of the Dutch and English navies. It is possible to see the extent to which the relaunch of the project for the canal between "*les Deux Mers*" (the Two Seas) was very much part of Colbert's logic: greater activity for the port of Bordeaux, opening up of Toulouse, increase in trade in agricultural products from the Lauragais region (south of Toulouse) to the Mediterranean basin, relaunch of the ports of the eastern Mediterranean – Aigues-Mortes and Agde no longer played a role because of the encroaching sand and, for the same reason, access to Frontignan, was forbidden to high tonnage ships, and the port infrastructure in Sète, commenced in the reign of Henri IV, had been abandoned owing to a lack of funds – and, finally, isolation of the Spanish enemy, which would be deprived of part of its revenue from the transit of maritime traffic through the Gibraltar Straits.

The desire was there, all that remained was to resolve the technical problems, which had confounded the very best engineers over the past twenty centuries, and find ways to finance such a huge construction project, which wealthy empires and kingdoms had considered to be beyond their means. It is to one man that we owe all these answers, Pierre-Paul Riquet, certainly a high ranked civil servant, but not an engineer, or a hydrologist, a man without any diplomas, or even any serious academic background – he barely knew how to read Latin at a time when mastery of this language was vital for a man of average culture – a small-time provincial notable who laid claim, without any real evidence, to a very ancient lineage of Italian nobility, but whose true great asset, apart from his extraordinary intellectual, human and mental qualities, was the sizeable fortune inherited from his father, which, turning a blind eye to scruples, he used to yield a huge profit which he then poured into what was to become his lifetime's work.

The first obstacle to creating a waterway between the Atlantic and the Mediterranean was the irregular supply of water in the rivers – particularly the Aude and the Ariège – likely to be linked to the Garonne, and the fact that their poor potential for navigation meant that they were incapable of ensuring permanent traffic. But the most serious problem was the crossing of the Seuil de Naurouze, the highest point in the corridor of plains running between the Pyrenees and the Massif Central, where, there was no river with enough water to supply the canal. All previous projects – the Aude-Garonne junction in the reign of François I, the

The genius of the Two Seas

Portrait of Riquet.
Toulouse, Paul-Dupuy Museum. Inv. No. D.61.6.29. Photo STC.

Pierre-Paul Riquet was born in Béziers at an unknown date, maybe in 1604, but, more probably in 1609 since, on his death certificate (he died in 1680), he was declared to be 71 years of age. He was the eldest son of Guillaume Riquet, a notary and, later, a prosecutor in Béziers, but, above all, a businessman who, owing to the speed with which he accrued an enormous fortune, was considered for many long years to be of dubious reputation. The Riquet family claimed to be the descendants of a certain Gherardo Arrighetti, a Florentine aristocrat exiled in France at the end of the 13th century for having chosen the side of the Ghibellines, over the Guelphs who were victorious in his home town. This name is said to have been changed to Riquetti, then Riquety and finally Riquet. However, the authenticity of this lineage has never been established formally. After relatively short and succinct studies and an early marriage – he was just 19 years old when he married Catherine de Milhau – Pierre-Paul Riquet entered the salt tax administration services thanks to his father's influence and money. Energetic, obstinate, daring, enthusiastic, inquisitive, observant and imaginative – all qualities which reached their peak during the fifteen years it took to build the canal – he had a brilliant career. Firstly, as sous-fermier (assistant) of Haut Languedoc, then assistant farmer general of Languedoc, Roussillon and Cerdagne, he quickly built up a large fortune, which later helped to increase the already very lucrative income as arms supplier to the armies of the King of Catalonia. In 1651, he was still only the sous-fermier des Gabelles (salt tax administration), but, nevertheless, he was rich enough to buy the Lord's estate of Bonrepos near Verfeil, north-east of Toulouse, comprising 150 hectares of land and a Renaissance castle which he had demolished in 1660 in order to rebuild another following the architectural fashion of the time. How did the ancient project of a junction between the Two Seas come to obsess him to such an extent that he was prepared to risk his own fortune and that of his descendants? Nobody knows... Only some suggestions may be made. Often, he found himself in the Montagne Noire region, either in his role as the owner of land near Revel or in order to collect taxes. Maybe it was during one of these many walks that the idea of using the water from the rivers which flow down this mountain's slopes and channelling it to Naurouze came to him and never left him, even going so far assistant farmer general to become a lifetime obsession.

Obelisk dedicated to Paul Riquet at the Seuil de Naurouze.

Maybe, in his wish to complete a project which, until then, had been considered impossible, there was a desire to seek a form of social revenge which had not been quelled by his fortune but which only the recognition of his family pretensions to nobility could satisfy. Although Riquet never saw his work completed – by 4 kilometres and 6 months – and although to his heirs he left a fortune shattered into a thousand pieces and huge debts, at least, on his deathbed, he knew that his ingenuity was being hailed beyond the borders of the kingdom. And, his lifelong demand, passed on to him by his father, to rehabilitate the noble name of his lineage, was granted by Louis XIV in 1666: "... to treat favourably the aforementioned Riquet... his aforementioned majesty... declared and declares him to be noble... without him

Riquet presents his project to the King's commissioner.
Toulouse, Paul-Dupuy Museum. Inv. No. D.53.10.95. Photo STC.

Aude-Ariège junction in the reign of Henri IV – came up against these two problems, with the latter even being considered to be insurmountable.

Riquet's feat of ingenuity was finding the solutions to two problems. The whims of the River Aude are a handicap to regular traffic? Therefore, we must not use it as a navigable way and the canal must stretch as far as the Mediterranean. No river close to the watershed is able to ensure the canal's water supply? Then we shall capture the water which flows down the slopes of the Montagne Noire and lead them to reservoirs and, from there, through a system of channels, to the Seuil de Naurouze... This latter point was the most delicate: although the theory was attractive, it had to be verified on site that these mountain streams could be diverted and brought together in order to provide the volume of water required all year round. Accompanied by a water engineer, Pierre Campmas, Riquet systematically covered the entire Montagne Noire massif, identifying the waterways which, because of their orientation and flow, could be used – among the main ones retained were the Sor, the Laudot, the Rieutor, the Lampillon, the Lampy, the Bernassonne and the Alzau – then mapped the route of the future channels and defined the location of the "water reservoirs", of which he had initially planned about fifteen in a line along the main channel. He later bowed to the advice of Clerville's escort, one of the experts in charge of drawing up the quotation for the project, who suggested building just one large reservoir: this became Saint-Ferréol Lake, which, with its 64 hectares, was the largest manmade lake at that time. In order to check his ideas, he even went so far as to dig huge basins in his park at Bonrepos Castle, link them via an aqueduct and, with the help of models, carry out a series of experiments.

Stone bridge in the region of Carcassonne.

Saint-Ferréol Basin.
Toulouse, Paul-Dupuy Museum. Inv. No. 55.1.187. Photo STC.

The surroundings of the canal in the region of Preïssan.

Junction between the Ocean and the Mediterranean (Colbert presents the plan for the canal to Louis XIV)
Toulouse, Paul-Dupuy Museum.
Inv. No. 4.537. Photo STC.

Now convinced of the project's feasibility, and after having obtained, through diplomacy, the approval of a number of influential figures, such as the Bishop of Toulouse, Riquet decided to take the all-important step: in 1662, he sent a letter to Colbert "on the subject of a canal which could be built in this province of Languedoc to ensure communication between the Two Seas". It was barely a year since Louis XIV had proclaimed: "The State is me" and Colbert had just replaced Fouquet. The memo arrived at just the right time to attract the attention of a Minister who was looking to increase his own power through that of his King, and that of a monarch wishing to make an illustrious start to his reign with some major projects. Apart from the economic, political and strategic reasons already referred to, it was the technical arguments developed by Riquet which stimulated the interest of Colbert and Louis XIV leading to their decision to support the project. With prudence, they started by entrusting a commission with the role of examining its economic utility and feasibility. The appraisals started in January 1663 – this extraordinarily short timescale says as much about the importance of the opinion of the King and his Minister as the power of the belief conveyed in Riquet's memo and the effectiveness of his supporters in the provinces – and favourable reports followed. Before giving their final approval to the project, the commissioners were going to ask Riquet to give a real-life demonstration of the truth of his theory by digging a test channel between the Montagne Noire and the Seuil de Nauroze. The final test was completed successfully in October 1665: Riquet, who paid the 50,000 pounds required for the work from his own pocket, was now able to provide the ultimate proof that the problem of supplying water to the canal at the watershed had been well and truly resolved.

There remained the crucial issue of the funding for this project which promised to be the largest of the century. The quotation for the first phase of work, about one hundred kilometres between Toulouse and Trèbes, called the "first enterprise", was 3,630,000 pounds, an investment

Argeliers bridge in the region of Narbonne.

which the State, the coffers of which were almost empty, was unable to assume. This is where Riquet's other qualities came into play. This visionary and self-taught engineer was also an unequalled financer. The financial plan he came up with overcame the final hurdle: in exchange for a monopoly over the Languedoc *Fermes et Gabelles* for a ten-year period, and the raising of the status of the canal to a hereditary fief of which he would be Lord, with a right over justice, the perception of toll duties, the construction and sale of houses, shops and warehouses, he offered a partnership, undertaking to finance the work partly with his own money, the State and the province providing the complement, and to manage the project and see it through to completion. The contract appeared to favour Riquet, who, nevertheless, between the inevitable overrunning of budgets, continual delays by a bad-paying Administration and loans at exorbitant rates, was going to spend the rest of his life struggling against budgetary problems to such an extent that he sank his entire fortune in the project, namely about 3 million pounds, and even sacrificed his daughter's dowries to it. "I built a canal to drown myself and my entire family", he once said in a moment of despair. As a result, his descendants, the heirs to the fief, were going to continue to pay his debts - more than 2 million pounds - for almost half a century, before the canal ultimately started to make them hugely rich.

In October 1666, a Royal edict gave the order "that the construction of the navigation and communication canal of the Ocean and Mediterranean Two

The bridges over the Orb, the river which skirts the old town of Béziers.

Saint-Nazaire Cathedral and Pont Vieux in Béziers.

Decree for the construction of the canal.
VNF - South-western Regional Department - Canaux du Midi Archives. Photo Jean-Luc Auriol.

Seas be shortly undertaken..." At the age of 57, Pierre-Paul Riquet was ready to embark on his lifetime dream.

The work started on 15 April 1667 with the laying of the first stone of Saint-Ferréol Lake and was completed on 2 May 1681 with the priming of the last section ending in the Lagoon of Thau. Only fifteen years was needed to complete one of the most Herculean construction projects of the century. But, Riquet never saw the finished work: when he died on 1 October 1680, less than 4 kilometres remained to be completed to reach the Etang de Thau.

This astonishing speed considering the technical means of that time – the canal was dug with picks and spades, and 7 million cubic metres of earth and rubble were moved – owes everything to Riquet's exceptional organisational abilities. He had to manage a constantly changing workforce, partly comprising farmers who used to abandon the worksite during harvests and grape-picking. In order to compensate for this seasonal desertion, several times he had to commandeer soldiers before finally coming up with the idea of paying workers a monthly salary in order to encourage their loyalty. At the peak of the work, after 1670, there were as many as 12,000 workers, both men and women aged "from 20 years for the youngest to 50" divided up into "sections" of forty people, with two sections forming a "workshop" and one unit of twenty-five workshops being managed by a "general controller". The streamlining of work was pushed to an extreme: several worksites were in progress at the same time, on sites sometimes several dozen kilometres apart, which required a particularly effective communications system. For example, the construction of the port in Sète was in progress at the same time as the excavation of the section of the canal from Toulouse to Naurouze. The tasks assigned to the workers were of military precision: thus, in a section of 40 "heads" assigned to earthworks, there were "10 for digging, 10 for loading and 20 for moving earth".

It is all the more astonishing to see that Riquet had a true social conscience, relatively uncommon among *Fermiers de Gabelle* whose reputation for greed was not exaggerated. In effect, apart from the much higher than average salaries he paid to his workers – which could be explained by his need to ensure an abundant and

Section and elevation of the spillway-overflow channel Libron raft and bridge
Toulouse, Paul-Dupuy Museum. Inv. No. 67.31.23. Photo STC.

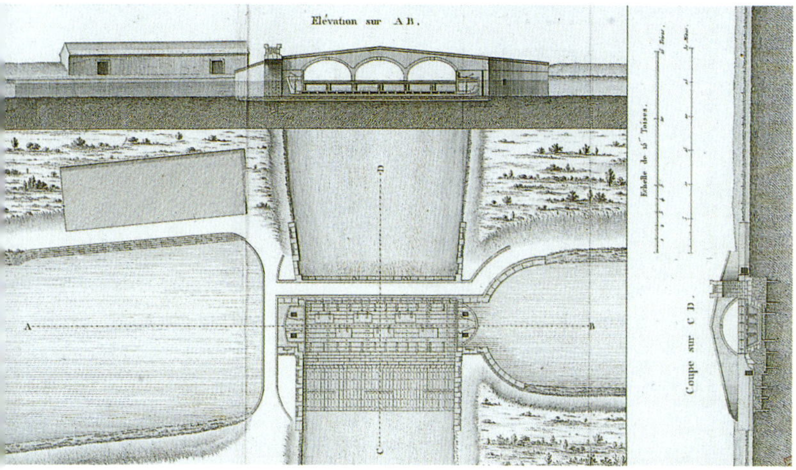

Entrance to Malpas tunnel
Toulouse, Paul-Dupuy Museum.
Inv. No. 63.237.18. Photo STC.

loyal workforce – he introduced social benefits almost unheard of at that time, such as payment for Sundays and public holidays, sick leave and even days paid when work had been suspended because of bad weather.

Managed in the same way as a rural army, engineers and workers helped the works to progress at an astonishing pace: in May 1668, namely eighteen months after the first stone was laid, the Toulouse-Naurouze section was primed and, in 1672, traffic along it was organised. In 1673, after many setbacks involving, among other things, the excavation of the port in Castelnaudary, the Naurouze-Trèbes section, too, was opened. However, the "second enterprise" – the Trèbes-Lagoon of Thau section – was going to be delayed by countless difficulties. Financial problems escalated: the province and State were reluctant to pay and the continuous overrunning of original quotations – in particular the number of locks which had been largely underestimated – was beginning to exasperate Colbert who was even starting to suspect Riquet of embezzling money, despite the fact that the latter was obliged not only to put almost all his belongings up for sale, but also to borrow hundreds of thousands of pounds. In this already unhealthy context, intrigues and malicious acts abounded: the town councillors of Narbonne, furious to learn that the route of the canal was going to pass through Béziers and not their own town mounted a campaign of denigration, and a second-in-command to Riquet, the engineer François Andréossy, tried to present himself to the King as the project's true creator and designer. To this were added technical problems, mainly resulting from the topography. At the cost of colossal work, Riquet exhausted himself overcoming obstacles sometimes said to be insurmountable and which he "effaced" with stupefying audacity: excavation of the Malpas tunnel, crossing of Cesse, Répudre canal-bridge, excavation of the longest reach ever attempted, construction of the Fonserannes "ladder". It is said that Colbert was tempted momentarily to order the closure of the construction works, despite their state of advancement. But, Riquet persisted and, in parallel, launched the "third enterprise", namely the construction of the port in Sète, chosen as the Mediterranean outlet for the canal after much hesitation, with Narbonne, which would have

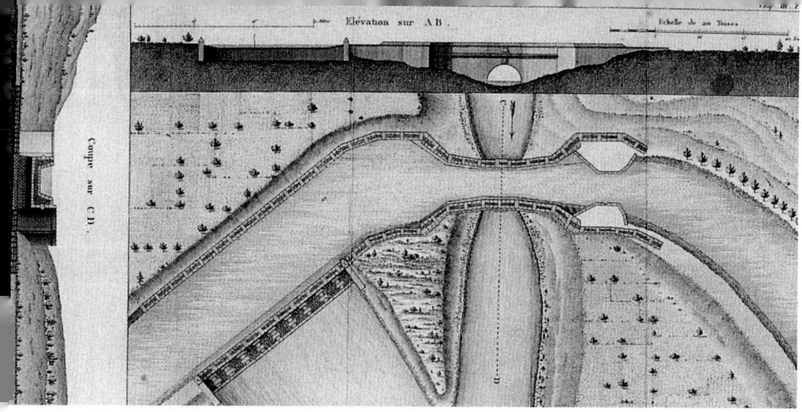

Plan, section and elevation of Repudre aqueduct
Toulouse, Paul-Dupuy Museum.
Inv. No. 67.31.17. Photo STC.

Louis XIV allegory
Toulouse, Paul-Dupuy Museum.
Inv. No. 53.85.1. Photo STC.

been linked to Port-la-Nouvelle, having played the role as main rival for many years. Started in 1666 with the rockfilling of Saint-Louis jetty, the work on the port of Sète was not completed until after Riquet's death and it was only in 1682 that the first ships were able to drop anchor at the quayside.

We know that, exhausted and ruined, Pierre-Paul Riquet never saw the completion of his work, which fell short by four miserable kilometres and six months of work. Nevertheless, during his fifteen year struggle with water and earth – and, even worse, against the sceptics, the envious, the usurpers and bad payers – he did enjoy huge satisfaction: that of being recognised in his lifetime as being a true genius: also that of being certain of leaving his name to one of the greatest construction projects of the 17th century; and, finally – although to us today it may appear relatively unimportant, but under the Ancien Regime, it was the ultimate prize – ennoblement and recognition by the King of the long lineage – although extremely doubtful – of his aristocratic ancestry.

"The Canal Joining the Two Seas is without doubt the most beautiful and most noble construction of its kind ever undertaken", wrote Vauban. This tribute – well-deserved and sincere – from one genius to another must not allow us to forget some of the harsher realities: pressed for time and hampered by cash flow problems, Riquet, concerned about working for future generations, demanded the use of the most noble and long-lasting materials even at the worst times of financial crisis, but, sometimes had to opt for more hasty solutions: thus several waterways crossed the canal over simple roadways and their spates regularly led to silting up and sanding over, resulting in high maintenance costs. Also, with the capacity of Saint-Ferréol Lake proving to be insufficient, the height of its dyke and its supply system needed to be reviewed.

It was to Vauban that Riquet's heirs turned to resolve these difficulties and correct these imperfections. While affirming "that he would have preferred the glory of being the author of the works to all that he had done or may do in the future", the one who, for almost ten years, was the "Commissioner of the Kingdom's Fortifications" was going to lead a huge campaign of work between 1687 and 1693: the dyke of Saint-Ferréol Lake was raised, and its water flow was regulated by the extension by more than 7 kilometres of the Montagne channel, which, among other things, involved the construction of Cammazes tunnel; forty-nine aqueducts and canal-bridges were built – among them the very spectacular ones of Cesse, Argentdouble, Orbiel and Pechlaurier – thus enabling the abandonment of the roadways with their tendency to sand up. But, these were only improvements – which Riquet had often imagined without having the means or the time to carry them out – and not a questioning of the construction's overall design.

Although river navigation between the Two Seas was now possible, certain things were still lacking and there were still several hurdles to overcome. In terms of what was missing, several major towns were not served, such as Carcassonne, which had refused the canal's passage before later regretting its decision, and Narbonne, which lost out to Béziers and Sète.

The junction with the River Rhone, although vital to the coherence of the project, was still only in its early stages. In terms of hurdles, the section between Toulouse and Bordeaux continued to follow the River Garonne. However, this river's capricious water flow, its violent spates, its ever-changing shallows and the boats, which were designed to navigate on the canal and could not use it, made a transfer of load necessary, as costly in time as it was in money.

Two more centuries were needed for Riquet's work to be completed and for it to be possible to truly talk about the canal (although canals would be more appropriate) of the Two Seas, with the Canal du Midi being a simple link in a much larger chain comprising a vast network of manmade waterways.

Narbonne was passed through by the Robine, a former bed of the River Aude which had already been turned into a canal in the Middle Ages and which was put back into service shortly after the opening of the Canal du Midi. But, it was only at the end of

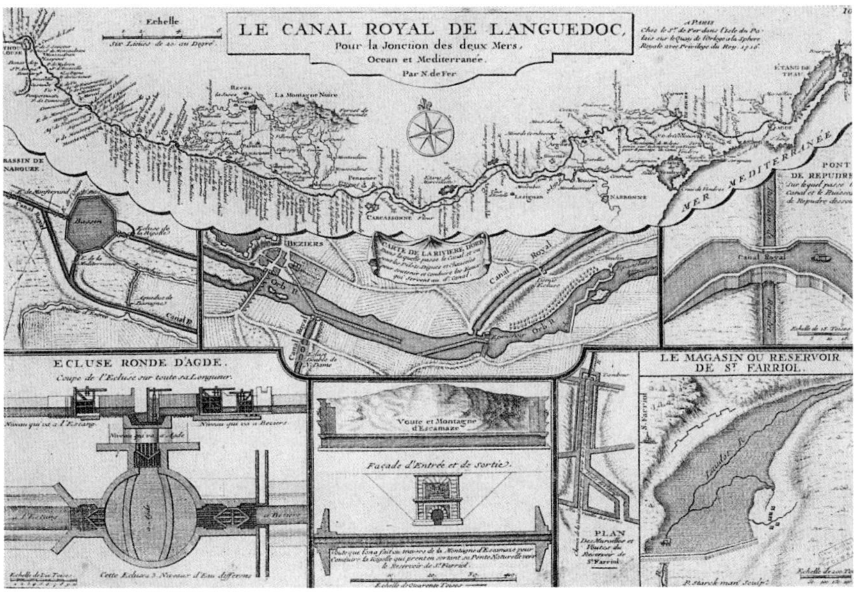

The Royal canal of Languedoc
Toulouse, Paul-Dupuy Museum.
Inv. No. 1.749. Photo STC.

Toulouse, the city and the quaysides of the Garonne. (Print, End of 19th century).

the 18th century that the creation of the junction canal – 5 kilometres between Port-la-Robine and Gailhousty – was going to allow the town to be linked to the Canal du Midi at long last. It was at the same time that Toulouse inaugurated the Canal de Brienne, a short construction – about 1.5 kilometres – but of great utility, because it provided a deviation around the Chaussée de Bazacle, one of the worst obstacles on the river as it passes through the city. In 1808, the junction between the River Rhone and the Lagoon of Thau, too, was completed with the extension as far as Beaucaire of the canal created at the end of the 17th century between Sète and Aigues-Mortes. In 1810, the Canal du Midi reached Carcassonne, in particular thanks to the construction of the Fresquel canal bridge. The last page was turned in 1857 when, after twenty-seven years of work, the Canal Latéral à la Garonne – 193 kilometres between Toulouse and Castets en Dorthe – was finally inaugurated. By then, a barge departing from Beaucaire could reach Bordeaux solely along manmade waterways, but, as chance would have it, it was exactly at the time that the Two Seas were, at long last, linked by a complete and coherent series of navigable waterways that rail and, then later, road transport started to flourish and compete with inland waterway transport before gradually killing it... The traffic on the canal peaked in the second half of the 19th century, before starting its irremediable decline, despite a slight recovery after the First World War. In 1989, the Canal du Midi's last commercial barge completed its final journey. Being of very little interest apart from for irrigation purposes, the Two Seas

Fresquel Lock, in the region of Carcassonne, with its incurved side walls, a typical form of architecture desired by Riquet.

Canal Latéral à la Garonne (photograph).
Toulouse, Paul-Dupuy Museum. Inv. No. 64.3.2. Photo STC.

canal was threatened with complete abandonment, however, salvation came with the recent new fashion for river tourism. The some 100,000 people who travel along the canals every year aboard hundreds of small barges, ten hotel-boats and more than five hundred private boats, to which are added the countless walkers and cyclists who follow the towpaths, have provided these waterways with a genuine economic interest. In 1996, the listing of the Canal du Midi as a World Heritage Site not only marked the universal recognition of Riquet's ingenuity, but, without doubt, also ensured that his work will be passed on intact to future generations.

Riquet's heirs

On Riquet's death, it was his two sons, Jean-Mathias, Baron of Bonrepos, and Pierre-Paul, Count of Caraman, who took over ownership of the canal, now a hereditary fief. Intelligent management and the sale of part of the company's assets enabled them to refund gradually their father's debts – although as we already saw, this took more than forty years – and to earn considerable revenue from the canal from the first third of the 18th century to the Revolution. In 1792, with the Caraman family having emigrated, the Republic confiscated the canal. Riquet's descendants had to wait until the Restoration to recover part of their assets, but only for a short while, since, competition from rail led to an increasingly marked decline in traffic and, therefore, in benefits. In 1858, a decree signed by Napoleon III entrusted the management of the canal for a period of ten years to its most dangerous enemy, the Compagnie des Chemins de Fer du Midi, the owner of the brand new railway line from Bordeaux to Narbonne. It was the start of an agonising death. When the concession came to an end in 1898, the State bought all the shares in the canal, which, as a result, found itself nationalised. Its status has never changed since, and, since 1991, its management has been entrusted to the Administration of the Voies Navigables de France.

The Canal du Midi in figures

240 kilometres long.
1.60 metres average theoretical depth,
1.40 metres average practical depth.
20 metres average at water level,
11 metres average at ceiling level.
Minimum size of locks: 30 metres long by 5.35 metres wide.
Highest point: 190 metres in altitude at the Seuil de Naurouze.
Altitude difference between Toulouse and the Seuil de Naurouze: 58 metres.
Altitude difference between the Seuil de Naurouze and the Etang de Thau: 110 metres.
350 constructions, of which 126 bridges, 55 aqueducts, 6 dams,
7 canal bridges.
63 locks, of which 1 septuple, 1 quadruple, 4 triples and 19 doubles.
Number of trees originally planted on the banks: 45,000.
Current number of trees: about 60,000.
Longest reach: 53.490 kilometres between Argens Lock and Fonserannes Lock.
Shortest reach: 250 metres between the two Fresquel Locks.

ADMINISTRATION DU CANAL DU MIDI

Direction TRANSPORTS Accélérés — Service d'AGEN Beaucaire

Marques | N° | Poids | Colis | Désignation — Toulouse, le 20 ... 185.

Travel ticket Accelerated transport department – Agen Service in Beaucaire.
Toulouse, Paul-Dupuy Museum. Inv. No. 4.479. Photo STC.

The most used lock: Argens, 11,000 boats a year carrying an average of 5 passengers.
Number of hectares irrigated by the canal: 24,000.
Number of direct jobs resulting from the canal: 1,009.
Annual economic revenue from the activity of the Two Seas canal: about 800 million Francs (€122 million).

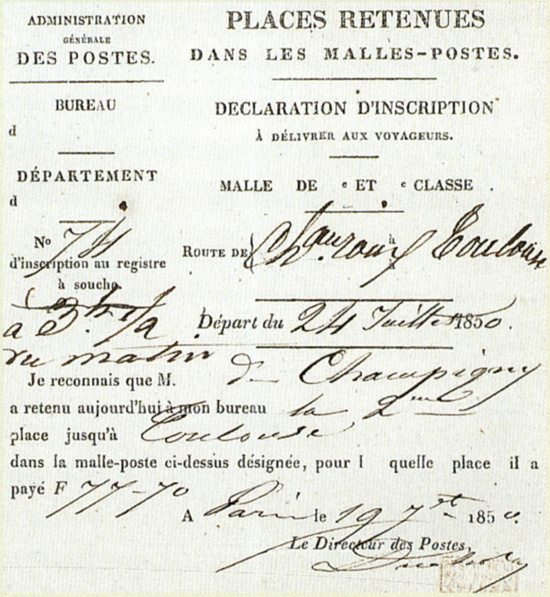

ADMINISTRATION GÉNÉRALE DES POSTES.

PLACES RETENUES DANS LES MALLES-POSTES.

BUREAU d

DÉCLARATION D'INSCRIPTION À DÉLIVRER AUX VOYAGEURS.

DÉPARTEMENT d

MALLE DE e ET e CLASSE.

No 741 d'inscription au registre à souche.

ROUTE DE ... à Toulouse

Départ du 24 Juillet 1850.

Je reconnais que M. ... a retenu aujourd'hui à mon bureau la 2e place jusqu'à Toulouse dans la malle-poste ci-dessus désignée, pour laquelle il a payé F 77-70

A Paris le 19 7bre 185..

Le Directeur des Postes.

Reserved seats in the mail coach (recto).
Toulouse, Paul-Dupuy Museum. Inv. No. 70.4.1. Photo STC.

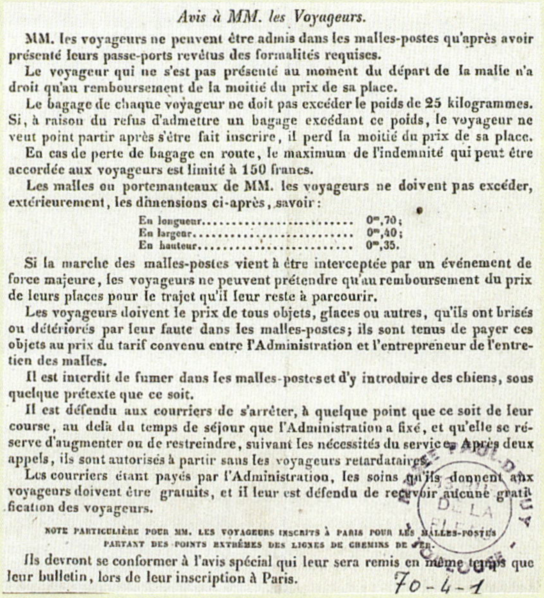

Avis à MM. les Voyageurs.

MM. les voyageurs ne peuvent être admis dans les malles-postes qu'après avoir présenté leurs passe-ports revêtus des formalités requises.

Le voyageur qui ne s'est pas présenté au moment du départ de la malle n'a droit qu'au remboursement de la moitié du prix de sa place.

Le bagage de chaque voyageur ne doit pas excéder le poids de 25 kilogrammes. Si, à raison du refus d'admettre un bagage excédant ce poids, le voyageur ne veut point partir après s'être fait inscrire, il perd la moitié du prix de sa place.

En cas de perte de bagage en route, le maximum de l'indemnité qui peut être accordée aux voyageurs est limité à 150 francs.

Les malles ou portemanteaux de MM. les voyageurs ne doivent pas excéder, extérieurement, les dimensions ci-après, savoir :

En longueur .... 0m,70 ;
En largeur .... 0m,40 ;
En hauteur .... 0m,35.

Si la marche des malles-postes vient à être interceptée par un événement de force majeure, les voyageurs ne peuvent prétendre qu'au remboursement du prix de leurs places pour le trajet qu'il leur reste à parcourir.

Les voyageurs doivent le prix de tous objets, glaces ou autres, qu'ils ont brisés ou détériorés par leur faute dans les malles-postes; ils sont tenus de payer ces objets au prix du tarif convenu entre l'Administration et l'entrepreneur de l'entretien des malles.

Il est interdit de fumer dans les malles-postes et d'y introduire des chiens, sous quelque prétexte que ce soit.

Il est défendu aux courriers de s'arrêter, à quelque point que ce soit de leur course, au delà du temps de séjour que l'Administration a fixé, et qu'elle se réserve d'augmenter ou de restreindre, suivant les nécessités du service. Après deux appels, ils sont autorisés à partir sans les voyageurs retardataires.

Les courriers étant payés par l'Administration, les soins qu'ils donnent aux voyageurs doivent être gratuits, et il leur est défendu de recevoir aucune gratification des voyageurs.

NOTE PARTICULIÈRE POUR MM. LES VOYAGEURS INSCRITS À PARIS POUR LES MALLES-POSTES PARTANT DES POINTS EXTRÊMES DES LIGNES DE CHEMINS DE FER.

Ils devront se conformer à l'avis spécial qui leur sera remis en même temps que leur bulletin, lors de leur inscription à Paris.

70-4-1

Reserved seats in the mail coach (verso).
Toulouse, Paul-Dupuy Museum. Inv. No. 70.4.1. Photo STC.

Transport on the canal in former times

After its completion in 1681, the Canal du Midi became a major communication route used as much for carrying goods as passengers. Although sea boats travelled along it in both directions, with their masts folded, in order to avoid Gibraltar, it was specially designed, locally built ships which formed the bulk of the fleet. For carrying freight, boats measuring about twenty metres in length were used, towed by men or horses and able to carry as much as 120 tons.
Until the middle of the 19th century, there were between 200 and 250 of these boats navigating on the canal simultaneously. The freight mainly comprised cereals, wine, fruit and dried fish and, sometimes, in times of war, troops, weapons and cannon. Between Sète and Toulouse, the average journey time for boats with the heaviest loads was about eight days.
Passengers used to occupy the "mail carriages" towed by horses in the same way as the barges, the comfort and speed of which continued to improve over the years. Initially, they were small in size – about a dozen metres long – and only offered a rough shelter on the bridge. But, very quickly, they became more imposing – up to 30 metres long – and were equipped with a large furnished lounge with windows opening out over the passing landscapes. This did not mean that the journey was restful: for more than a century, in order to save time, the many locks were not passed through and travellers were transferred with their luggage from one "carriage" to another. To these many transfers – there are twenty-five multiple locks between Toulouse and the Lagoon of Thau – was added stops for lunch, "la dînée" and another for the night stopover in an inn close to a lock because navigation was not possible at night. Despite all this, only four days were needed to cover the canal's 240 kilometres. From the start of the 19th century, competition from stagecoaches, and then, later, from rail, encouraged the canal's managers to do everything possible to improve passenger comfort and shorten journey time. "(...) a lounge, corresponding in some respects to a first class rail carriage, is created at the front of the post boat for "travellers of distinction", whereas a common room, at the rear, served as second class. Meal stops were planned in Castelnaudary, Carcassonne and Somail, and also, restaurants were created on board[1]". "Express" boats were put into

View of the Redorte curve
Toulouse, Paul-Dupuy Museum.
Inv. No. 67.67.3. Photo STC.

service, towed by trotting horses led by a postilion and replaced every eight kilometres. Transfers at the many locks were done away with – except in Fonserannes – and night navigation was authorised.
Journey times started to fall: by the middle of the century only 32 hours were needed to travel from Toulouse to Sète – almost 100 hours were needed a century earlier – "which represents an hourly speed of about 11 kilometres. Our self-propelled barges are far from achieving that today. Speed increased rapidly in the following years to reach 17 kilometres by about 1860... exactly at the same time as the mail boat disappeared[1]."

1. *"Connaissance du Canal du Midi"*, Arnaud d'Antin de Vaillac, Éd. France-Empire.

The Canal du Midi, from Toulouse to the Seuil de Naurouze

In which direction should you follow the canal's 240 kilometres? From Toulouse to Sète, or the other way? You may hesitate... You may think that it is not important because, in all cases, you will encounter the same landscapes, cross the same locks and stop at the same towns. But, do not be mistaken, because it is important to choose well. If we have chosen to depart from Toulouse, there are a few reasons for this. The first is historical: it was from west to east that the canal was built, even though, as we have seen, several

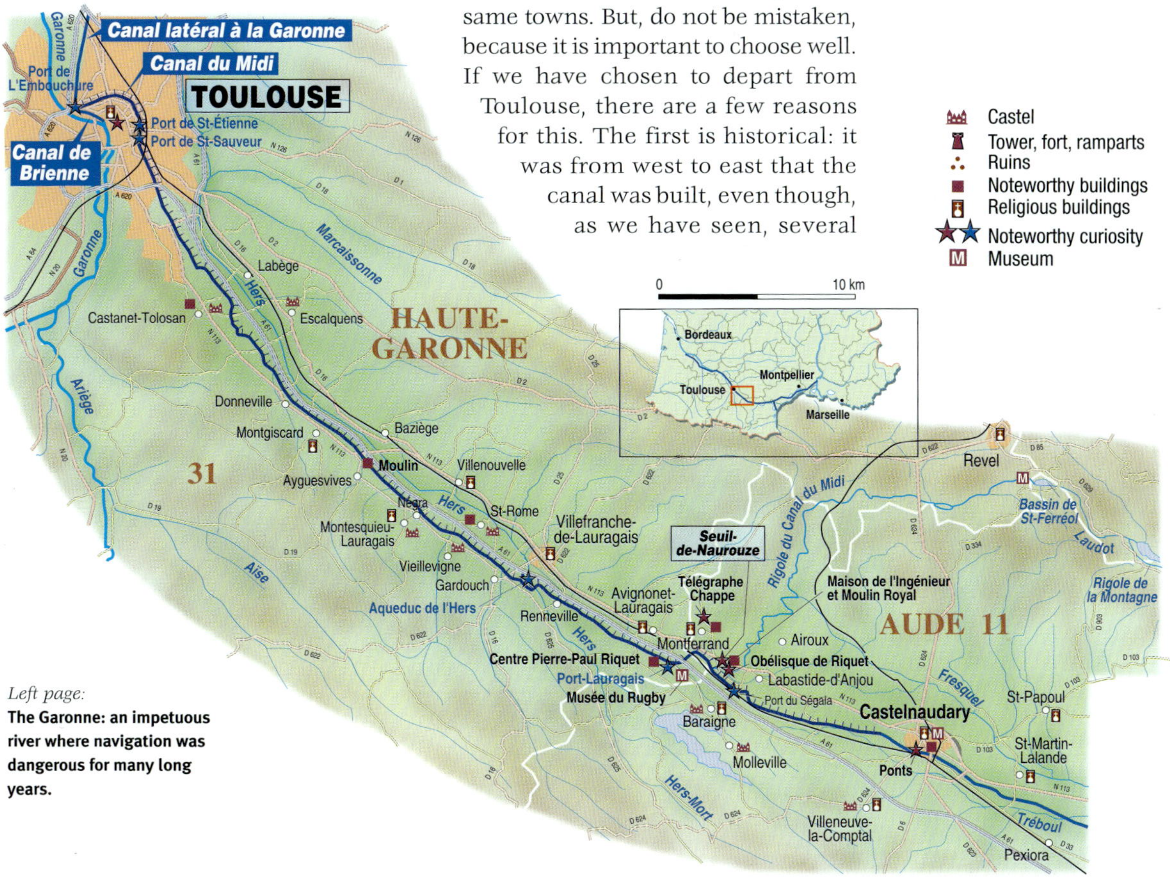

Left page:
The Garonne: an impetuous river where navigation was dangerous for many long years.

Toulouse.
Boulevard Riquet
and the Canal du Midi.

The Japanese garden
in Toulouse.

worksites were in progress at the same time. Therefore, following the route designed by Riquet in almost chronological order, encountering, in the same way as him, the difficulties which he had to overcome, all help contribute to a better understanding of the scale of his work. The second is purely subjective: even if a canal is not a river, even if it does not "flow" from a source to an outlet, is not travelling towards the sea a way of following the natural course of things? And, the last reason is not the least important:

Toulouse.
The Canal du Midi.
The Negreneys footbridge.

The Montagne Noire Saint-Ferréol Basin and dyke (Tarn) on a public holiday (postcard)
Toulouse, Paul-Dupuy Museum.
Inv. No. D.55.4.1293. Photo STC.

A barge at Saint-Etienne port, on the Canal du Midi, in Toulouse.

spending time in the hustle and bustle of one of the liveliest cities in France only makes the contrast with the peace and silence to be tasted over the ensuing days and nights between the banks of this huge waterway all the more exquisite.

From Toulouse to the Seuil de Naurouze, the canal passes through the rich countryside of Lauragais, in this "furrow", which, since ancient times, situated between the foothills of the Pyrenees and the southern slopes of the Massif Central, has always been a centre for passage and exchanges. The birthplace of a brilliant and refined civilisation, ravaged to its core by the terrible repression of Catharism, but still a land of good living and good eating, a fertile region made rich by pastel and then by cereals, Lauragais, with its luminous landscapes, its pink brick towns, its bastides and castles is still very much this "land of plenty", the

The Canal de Brienne, in Toulouse, links the Canal du Midi to the Garonne.

The Salle Illustres in Capitole (Toulouse city hall).

beauty, prosperity and culture of which fascinated the whole of Europe for many years.

No need to state the obvious: intelligent, cultured, young, cosmopolitan, filled with laughter, spirit and music, Toulouse is stunning. Firstly, because it is well and truly – apologies for the banality – the "*ville rose*" (pink city) boasted about in tourist brochures. It is true that it is also red when the sky darkens, or purple in the light of the setting sun, but above all, it is pink, with its pink roofs, walls and lights. Pink in the image reflected in the waters of the Garonne and the canals, pink even in the heart of the night under the light of the street lamps. However much you are in a hurry to cast off and set sail, give the city a little of the time it so rightly deserves, not only for its monuments – the Place du Capitole, Saint-Sernin Basilica, the Couvent des Jacobins and Saint-Étienne Cathedral – but also, and it is only in this way that you will understand it fully, in order to spend many hours strolling around its streets. Very few towns have been associated with so many stereotypes, rugby, Cassoulet, Airbus, goose confit, Nougaro, and many more... In the eyes of the French, Toulouse's identity is relatively unclear and even ambivalent: both very much a French-style city of a kind reserved for a Basque beret-wearing indigenous population with a thick accent, and a high-tech centre peopled by engineers dressed in white coats who, in secret, are preparing the world of the 3rd millennium. It could be said that it is too much for one city, but not for Toulouse: Futuropolis, it is; Count's capital it remains. And, even if it has known how to preserve the best of these two roles: not a museum-town – it is too young and lively for that – or a Houston-on-Garonne – it is made of a civilisation far too old to fall into that trap – spending a few hours or a few days there means constantly encountering these two contradictory realities which some strange form of chemistry has made harmonious. There is the picturesque medieval district, the formality inspired by the Renaissance townhouses, the hidden and silent courtyards glimpsed beyond porches, the shady banks of the canals, the unusual-shaped small squares, the

The banks of the Garonne seen from Place de la Daurade in Toulouse.

quaysides and the fountains. But, there are also traffic jams to make Parisians blanch, noisy terraces of student bars and laboratories where spacemen work. That is why it is a pity to leave this superb and paradoxical city without having enjoyed a taste of all its flavours. From the canal, which forms a large curve around it, it is easy to walk to the city's most interesting neighbourhoods. Drop anchor first of all at the port of Embouchure. Although slightly noisy – a very busy bypass runs alongside it – the site is superb. This vast body of water – 240 metres long – built in 1670 and extended in the 18th and 19th centuries, is the point at which the Canal du Midi joins the Canal de Brienne and the Canal Latéral à la Garonne. Although, sadly, Riquet's works have disappeared, the "Ponts Jumeaux", built in 1774 over the Canal du Midi

The Hotel d'Assézat, built during the period when pastel was making the fortune of Toulouse.

The violet

You may be surprised to discover that this flower, which is the symbol of modesty, is linked to the name of the proud Occitan capital. But this is the case. In former times, there only were violets from Toulouse. It is said that this plant was carried from Parma by soldiers fighting in Italy under Bonaparte.
The public's infatuation was immediate: perfectly suited to the climate, it was adopted by florists and horticulturists, distilled by perfume makers and turned into delicious sweets by confectioners. At the start of the century, this blue-purple winter flower – it is picked from October to March – largely contributed to the city's economy. However, after the First World War, difficulties in finding a workforce and the appearance of diseases specific to the plant led progressively to the collapse of production. Recovery only dates from 1985, when research enabled its culture in vitro. For the past ten or so years, greenhouse production has resumed. Without reaching the levels of former times, it is now, nevertheless, sufficient for the violet, once again to be considered as the emblem of the pink city.

© Sclaresky Monique.

Embouchure port in Toulouse, where the Canal du Midi, the Brienne Canal and the Canal Latéral à la Garonne meet.

and the Canal de Brienne, completed in 1843 by a third with the construction of the Canal Latéral, form a beautiful ensemble.

The port of Embouchure is the ideal starting point for a walk along the Canal de Brienne and along the right bank of the Garonne. To visit the city centre, you may, after having passed the Béarnais Lock and the Minimes Lock and passed a final reach with its banks occupied by a stunning garden, drop anchor upstream of Bayard Lock, about 3.5 kilometres from the port of Embouchure, not far from a statue of Riquet and the bridge which bears his name. From there, the main monuments and the city's oldest neighbourhoods are easily accessible on foot or by bicycle.

Between Bayard and Castanet Locks, the canal passes through the south-eastern neighbourhoods and suburbs of Toulouse. Despite the presence of a few interesting constructions, such as Saint-Étienne port, near which stands an 18th century cereal market, Saint-Sauveur port, where a few installations from the 18th century still remain, the rare Ramonville pas-

The canals in Toulouse. Saint-Pierre Lock, Canal de Brienne (postcard)
Toulouse, Paul-Dupuy Museum. Inv. No. D.53.16.919. Photo STC.

Toulouse, the Colonnes des Minimes. Group of washerwomen at the Canal (postcard).
Toulouse, Paul-Dupuy Museum.
Inv. No. D.53.16.1993. Photo STC.

tel mill (see inset) and, finally, Madron port and aqueduct built by Vauban, nothing will be lost if you choose to cover this long reach – more than 12 kilometres – relatively quickly, even if, from the Herbettes canal bridge (P.K. 8), the landscapes open out and become more rural. However, do take a break at Castanet Lock – the first one which Riquet gave an ovoid shape, a model which was employed for all the locks – and visit Castanet-Tolosan (1.5 kilometres) which has two interesting monuments: the *Vieil Hôpital* (Old Hospital) – 13th and 17th centuries – and the Medieval and Renaissance Rabaudy Castle.

After Castanet Lock, the canal's route becomes more sinuous, but, unfortunately, never leaves the N 113 main road and the A 61 motorway, which follow its course.

Therefore, it is best to quickly pass through the reaches, respectively 1.710 kilometres and 7.490 kilometres, between Vic and Montgiscard Locks, although the very beautiful brick castle (13th-16th century) in Escalquens, 2.5 kilometres from Vic, is well worth a visit. This is also the case with Mont-

Toulouse, the Minimes Locks (postcard).
Toulouse, Paul-Dupuy Museum.
Inv. No. 62.83.1102. Photo STC.

Escalquens Castle (13th – 16th century) typical Toulouse-style architecture.

On the right below:
Négra Lock, the site of the first day's "dînée" lunch stop.

Montgiscard.
The Lock on the Canal du Midi.

giscard, situated on the canal's right bank: this former bastide has a superb 14th century Gothic church with a bell gable with six bays which is a masterpiece of Toulouse architecture.

The following reaches – 3.207, 1.502 and 3.662 kilometres – lead successively to Ayguesvives Lock – where there is a mill dating from 1831 – Sanglier Lock and Négra Lock. Make a stopover at the last lock, in the same way as 17th century travellers did, since it was here that the first "*dînée*" – meaning lunch – was taken by passengers travelling on the "mail carriage" from Toulouse. They actually landed in a proper small village, a distant ancestor of today's motorway service stations, where they were offered a choice of facilities: hotels, restaurants and places of worship. The buildings have been preserved and it is still possible to see the chapel, the stables for the tow-horses and the small houses where the dining rooms were installed. From Négra, take a trip to two beautiful villages situated within easy reach of the canal: firstly, Montesquieu-Lauragais (1 kilometre) with its two

castles, one built in the Renaissance and redesigned in the 19th century and the other built entirely in the 19th century, and its brick church (16th century); then Villenouvelle (2 kilometres), for the superb bell gable of its 16th century church. Upstream from Négra, drop anchor near P.K. 35. On the right bank, Vieillevigne (1 kilometre) offers a sumptuous 15th century castle as well as a very beautiful view over the Hers Plain and, on a clear day, the Pyrenees. On the left bank, Saint-Rome (2 kilometres) is a curiosity in the region: at the end of the last century, a certain Louis-César de la Panouse, an architecture enthusiast with some crazy ideas, had a sort of ideal city built where he wanted to bring together the farmers, artisans and agricultural workers from his estates with a view to creating a strange type of seigneurial community. The castle and the twenty or so buildings built around it offer a strange assortment of styles, from Moorish to Palladian, Flemish to Neo-Byzantine, not to mention Baroque and Tudor. However, the site tends to inspire stupor rather than admiration because of its strangeness, on a par with the work of the Facteur Cheval.

After these visits, we will continue along the canal to cross the Laval and Gardouch Locks to stop at P.K. 42, between Lers Aqueduct – one of the most beautiful on the route, built in

The bell gable of Villenouvelle Church (16th century) is one of the most beautiful in the region of Toulouse.

Top left:
Montesquieu-Lauragais, the ancient capital of pastel.

Moorish building on the former estate of the Marquis of La Panouse in Saint-Rome.

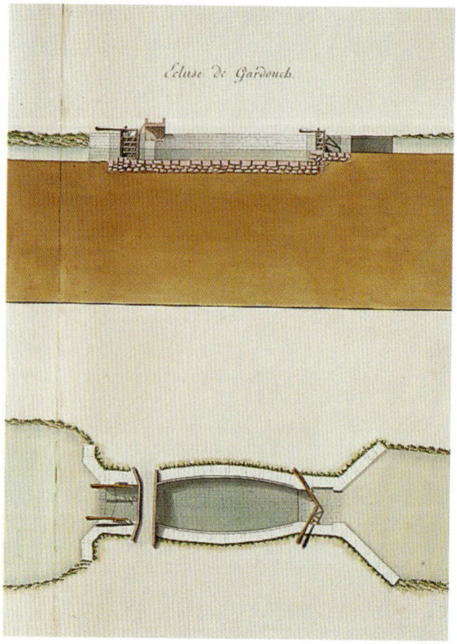

Plan and section of Gardouch Lock.
VNF - South-western Regional Division - Archives des Canaux du Midi.
Photo Jean-Luc Auriol.

1686 under the orders of Vauban – and Renneville Lock. About 1 kilometre further along, Villefranche-de-Lauragais is a delightful small town which was at its zenith in the 16th century when pastel made its fortune. The geometrical layout of its streets, characteristic of bastides, its *"pountets"* – passageways between the first floors of two houses – its flower-covered squares and gardens, and the beautiful pink brick buildings, including an outstanding Toulouse-style Gothic church, a remnant of the town's golden age, make it a delightful stopover.

Beyond Renneville, there are two locks to pass – Encassan and Emborrel – and 8 kilometres to be covered before a long stop at Port-Lauragais, situated alongside ... a huge motorway rest area. No, it is not a joke... There are two reasons for this being an umissable stopover, even if it is noisy and crowded. The first is cultural: the Pierre-Paul-Riquet Centre which presents the history of the building of the canal through plans, models and reproductions of ancient documents and audiovisual presentations, all of which is remarkably instructive. The Rugby Museum next-door is not only entertaining, but, above all, a must if you want to find out more about one of the major cults in this region of the oval ball. And, the large fountain which schematises the canal's water supply system and the functioning of the locks is very useful for understanding an incredibly complex system. The second reason is the presence, 1 kilometre from the port, of the small town of Avignonet-en-Lauragais, which offers an interesting transition: the brick so characteristic of Toulouse architecture disappears and is replaced by stone. Of its brilliant past – in the Middle Ages, it was a stronghold of the Viscounts of

The bell gable in Villefranche-de-Lauragais and its 16th century bells.

Pastel

It was thanks to this tinctorial plant, which grows wild in the countryside of Lauragais and Albigeois, that, from the middle of the 15th century to the 16th century, Toulouse experienced the period of greatest wealth in its history.
At that time, the blue dye extracted from this plant was highly fashionable throughout
Europe. The leaves of pastel, handpicked in June and July, were dried and ground and, after fermenting for six to eight weeks, the pulp was formed into balls about fifteen centimetres in diameter and weighing about 700 grammes, known as "coques", the origin of the name "pays de cocagne" given to the region of Toulouse. Placed under the shelter of a roof, the "coques" were left to dry in the open air until spring. They were then crushed and mixed with stagnant water, or even liquid manure or human urine. This thick and noxious mixture was left to ferment a second time for four to five months, during which time it gradually dried to become a thick and grainy paste, "agranat", the final step in obtaining the dye. One ton of leaves was needed to obtain 50 kilos of agranat... Although very hazardous, the culture and sale of pastel enabled dynasties of pastel traders – Boisson, Lancefoc, Bernuy, Assézat – not only to build up huge fortunes, as can be seen by the sumptuous townhouses which they had built in Toulouse, but also to obtain titles for themselves.
However, this golden age lasted barely a century: from 1560 onwards, the start of the Wars of Religion and competition from indigo which, imported from the colonies, proved itself to be cheaper and richer in dye, led to the demise of the pastel industry within the space of a few years. But, this glorious period of the "pays de cocagne" where "the more you sleep, the more you earn" has remained forever in people's memories. In recent years, the production of pastel has been relaunched and, although the activity is modest, it does allow a few artisans in Toulouse to offer fabrics dyed with extraordinary shades of blue which no other natural or artificial dye will ever be able to copy.

© Jacques

Pastel siliques and seeds.

© Tim Clinch

Henri Lambert, a master in the art of pastel.

Coque or cocagne.

© Tarn Departmental Tourism Committee

Lautrec and played a major role during the Albigensian Crusade before becoming one of the capitals of pastel – it has preserved the remains of the city wall, including a superb pepperbox tower and, above all, a Gothic church, Notre-Dame-des-Miracles, of admirable scale and purity.

Of course, we will arrange to leave behind the hustle and bustle of Port-Lauragais before nightfall, especially with one of the most beautiful and

The pepperbox tower (1606) in Avignonet-en-Lauragais: the main element of the village's fortifications, it also served as a prison.

Top:
The armed knight on the pepperbox tower offers a reminder of the massacres of the Albigensian Crusade.

Canal summit slab at the Naurouze sill.

most interesting sections of the canal being just a few minutes away.

Between the Océan Lock, slightly over 1,500 metres away, and the Méditerranée Lock, 5 kilometres further on, we are going to navigate – and, better still, drop anchor for a few hours – in the watershed reach, the existence of which was a condition for the entire canal and which offers a prime example of Riquet's ingenuity.

It is the pinnacle – in all meanings of the word – of his work: it is there – at an altitude of exactly 189.43 metres – that the canal reaches its highest point, where the waters from the Montagne Noire divide, following a line so exact that it is said that depending on which slope of the roof of the *Maison de l'Ingénieur* raindrops fell, they flowed either towards the Mediterranean or

Saint-Ferréol Lake

Without this 67-hectare manmade lake, situated 3 kilometres from Revel, the Canal du Midi would never have seen the light of day. Riquet's ingenious feat, you will recall, was to have come up with the idea of collecting water from the Montagne Noire to supply the upper reach at the Seuil de Naurouze. It is true that, originally, he had planned to create a line of fifteen basins and that the idea of creating only one of a much larger size should be attributed to Clerville's escort. What does it matter? Riquet's merit was to have known how to adopt solutions proposed by others when they appeared to be better.
Six years and a thousand workers equipped with spades, picks, wheelbarrows and baskets were needed to complete this giant construction project. The lake is supplied by the Montagne Channel, itself coming from Lampy Basin, and by the waters from the Laudot. The dam – 786 metres long and 149 metres wide – comprises three parallel walls, the upstream wall, the "large wall" – 35 metres high – and the downstream wall, surmounted with vaults with the spaces between them filled with rubble. A so-called "belt" channel surrounds part of the basin and enables the evacuation of water when it is emptied every ten years. As has been the canal, Saint-Ferréol Lake has been listed as a World Heritage Site. A Lake Museum, situated near the falls, presents the tools employed at the time of the canal's construction. This visit can be combined with a visit to the "voûte des robinets", between the upstream and downstream walls, where the basin's emptying system can be seen. With its beaches and its water sports centre, Saint-Ferréol Lake has become a major tourist attraction in the Toulouse region.
No doubt, it is a fate which Riquet had not imagined for it.

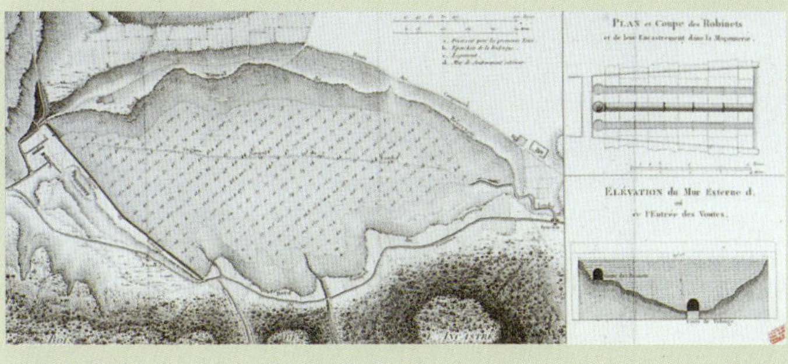

Plan of Saint-Ferréol reservoir. Toulouse, Paul-Dupuy Museum. Inv. No. 67.31.7. PhotoSTC.

Plaque on the Océan Lock at the Seuil de Naurouze.

The spectacular alley with 62 hundred-year old plane trees leading to the Océan Lock.

towards the Atlantic. It was there that, Riquet devised, searched for and finally found the key to the junction between the Two Seas.

The Seuil de Naurouze is not only a historic site, it is also an extraordinary world of peaceful beauty: the shady banks of the canal, the Arboretum planted with cedar, maple and aelppo pine, the spectacular alley lined with 62 plane trees – some exceeding 45 metres – and, above all, the magnificent state of conservation of the works of Riquet and Vauban – overflow channel, canal and locks – all make it a wonderful place to stop. Every year, an average of 30 million cubic metres of water are carried to the site along the Plaine Channel and discharged towards the Mediterranean or the Atlantic according to navigation needs, as well as irrigation networks. Originally, Riquet had dug a huge octagonal basin on the site, lined with dressed stone – 400 metres long, 300 metres wide and 3 metres deep – designed to stock some of the water required for the canal, around which he had planned to build a town, "... with small houses bearing a close resemblance to the model of Place Royale in Paris, a parish, an arsenal, shops for the boats". The town never saw the light of day – only a few service buildings were constructed – and, today, the location and contours of the basin, now filled in, can only be guessed at. When in use, it regularly silted up with alluvium from the channel and needed complete cleaning at least every two years at considerable

expense. It was finally abandoned in the middle of the 17th century.

It is only natural that the main monument erected in memory of Riquet is at the Seuil de Naurouze. Near the very beautiful *Maison de l'Ingénieur* – where the April 1814 armistice was signed between Soult and Wellington – and the *Moulin Royal* mill, a contemporary of the canal, a tree-lined alley leads to a 20-metre high obelisk resting on a sculpted pedestal, surrounded by a double ring of cedars, which the Caraman family, the direct descendants of the "Moïse du Languedoc", had built in 1825 in tribute to their grandfather. The natural base on which the monument rests has itself been a famous site since the Middle Ages. Legend has it that when the cracks which line the limestone of these "stones of Naurouze" close, it will be the end of the world.

Before leaving the watershed reach, do not miss out on a few short excursions. Firstly, to Montferrand (about 2 kilometres from the Océan Lock), an ancient Cathar fortress which, at an altitude of 300 metres, dominates the Seuil de Naurouze by about a hundred metres and offers not only a superb view over Lauragais and the Montagne Noire, but also some interesting remains: a 14th century fortified door, a 16th century bell gable, the Romanesque church of Saint-Pierre-d'Azonne, situated below, alongside the ruins of a palaeo-Christian basilica, and slightly unexpected in this medieval world, a Chappe telegraph tower, as well as a signal tower built in 1927 to guide Aéropostale pilots. Next, Baraigne, which, on the other side of the canal, less than 2 kilometres from Ségala port, has an impressive 15th,

Ganguise reservoir in the region of the Seuil de Naurouze: less than 5 kilometres from the canal, superb landscapes well worth the detour.

16th and 17th century castle and one of the most beautiful Romanesque churches (12th century) in the region. From this small town, the most courageous will not hesitate to cycle a further 2 kilometres through the superb landscapes of steep valleys flooded with lakes to admire the hilltop village of Molleville, dominated by the proud and imposing silhouette of its medieval castle.

From Toulouse to Ségala port, in the middle of the watershed reach, you will have covered 54 kilometres, passed fifteen locks, three of which are doubles, which have raised the level of the canal by a little more than 57 metres. The Méditerranée Lock is now going to open its doors for a slow descent – 190 kilometres, forty-eight locks and a 189-metre altitude difference – towards the Lagoon of Thau and Sète.

The Océan Lock, entrance to the watershed reach for boats coming from Toulouse.

"Perfects" and crusaders

Catharism – from the Greek word "katharos" meaning "pure" – and the terrifying repression of which its faithful were victims has made an ever-lasting mark in the history of the Southwest of France. There is barely a town or a village which does not still bear the remains of the massacres, pillaging and destruction which accompanied the crusades led by the Church, with the calculated support of the Kings of France who saw them as an opportunity to annex some wealthy territories.
Of this doctrine, originally from the Orient, we know that its main principle was the confrontation between Good and Evil.
God created an eternal Kingdom of the spirit governed by Good; Satan, because he invented matter and time, was at the origin of Evil; Man, who, through his body belonged to Evil and through his spirit to Good, had to fight to tear himself away from the world of Evil and gain access to the Kingdom of Good. Thus, he had to lead a life removed from all material concerns, devoting himself to poverty, chastity, humility and work, and practising fasting and vegetarianism, forbidding himself from killing, even animals. The "Bonshommes" or "Perfects" were those whom God had already brought back to the light and who had received the only recognised sacrament, the "consolamentum", both a baptism and an ordination. The "Believers" were simple followers still on the path of revelation.
They only received "consolamentum" on the point of death which, thus, was an equivalent of the extreme unction.

Unlike Catholicism, which excludes women from the priesthood, women played a major role in Catharism and many of the "Perfects" chose to form communities. Although the faithful were recruited mainly among traders and artisans, some important Lords converted – Raimond Roger, the Count of Foix, or Roger Trencavel, the Count of Béziers and Viscount of Carcassonne – or, at least, presented themselves as protectors of heresy, such as Raimond VI, the Count of Toulouse.
The Church was unable to ignore a doctrine which refuted certain sacraments – among others baptism and marriage – and openly criticised its wealth and the laxity of the ways of its clergy. In the middle of the 12th century, Saint Bernard came to preach to the Albigensians in an attempt to quell the rise of heresy. But, it continued to spread and, in 1208, Pope Innocent III seized the opportunity of the assassination of one of his legates, Pierre de Castelnau, to declare the first crusade against the Albigensians. The Knights of the North, to whom the Church had promised the same benefits as for a crusade in the Holy Land – absolution of sins, the promise of paradise for those who died in combat – arrived in droves from Champagne, Ile-de-France, Picardie, Flanders, and even Friesland and Rhineland, many of them dreaming of recovering fiefs in the rich southern provinces. Led initially by Simon de Montfort until his death in 1218, then by his son Amaury, the "holy war" lasted twenty years and was ruthlessly cruel. One example was the sacking of Béziers in 1209, when 30,000 inhabitants, men, women and children, were massacred. Cathar strongholds fell one after the other, but heresy was so far from being eradicated that a second crusade, led by the King of France Louis VIII, was declared by Pope Honorius III in 1226. In order to increase the effectiveness of the armed struggle, his successor, Gregory IX, created the Inquisition in 1233, and assigned its courts to track down and judge heretics. However, despite the means deployed, the Cathars resisted a further thirty years. Among the most famous events which marked this agonising death was the taking of Montségur: after a ten-month siege led by 6,000 crusaders, 215 heretics were burnt at the stake at the foot of the citadel. It was only in 1255, after the fall of Quéribus, their last stronghold, that the Cathars were finally defeated, at least on a military level because their religion continued to be practised in secret. It was thus that a "Perfect", Guillaume Bélibaste, was burnt alive in 1321, proof that heresy continued to have its supporters for many long years.
In 1271, Languedoc came under the authority of the Kingdom of France. After one of the longest and bloodiest wars of the Middle Ages, the North took control of the South and a refined and brilliant civilisation, the influence of which was felt throughout Europe, was extinguished.

Grandes chroniques de Saint-Denis.
Ancient documents from the time of the crusades against the Cathars and the Albigensians are extremely rare which is why this miniature from the Grandes Chroniques de Saint-Denis (around 1400) is so interesting; the stake is perhaps the object from the crusades which is the most present in the collective consciousness, especially when it not only concerned one person (as is the case here), but a group of several dozen, even several hundred "heretics".
Toulouse Municipal Library, Ms. 512, f° 251 r°, library photo.

From the Seuil de Naurouze to Trèbes

You have done it... The gates of the Méditerranée Lock have opened and from an "upstreamer" you have now become a "downstreamer". From brick to stone, from maize to vines, from Cassoulet to Loubine, from Castelnaudary to Carcassonne, Ensérune and Béziers, the route which awaits you offers so many superb landscapes, unforgettable towns, charming villages, castles, bastides, churches and abbeys, ingenious constructions by Riquet, gourmet temptations and curiosities, a journey through time, from Gallo-Roman Antiquity to the Middle Ages and the Renaissance, and it is so dizzying that two chapters will be needed to describe it.

Left page:
Most of the locks on the Canal du Midi are still operated by hand.

Next to some locks, actual villages were created to cater for travellers on the "mail carriage".

Downstream from the Méditerranée Lock, the hillier terrain made it necessary to considerably shorten the reaches. In fewer than 4 kilometres, we are going to pass through four locks – one a double and one a triple – for a total altitude difference of 17.23 metres. Beyond La Planque Lock, it is along a long reach – more than 4.5 kilometres – that you will arrive in Castelnaudary, one of the major stopovers on the canal, and certainly one of the most picturesque, and maybe even the one with the most delicious food.

According to the original plans, the canal never should have passed through this very ancient town, although it was very prosperous, with a large population and, also, the capital of the County of Lauragais. But Riquet, always on the lookout for new ways of funding his project, agreed to modify the route in exchange for a large contribution – 30,000 pounds – from the town's consuls. In actual fact, it proved to be an inspired move on their part: thanks to the excavation, between 1666 and 1671, of a

CASTELNAUDARY — Ecluses et Moulin St-Roch

View of Castelnaudary from the Grand Bassin, created by Riquet, which made the town's fortune.

huge basin – 7 hectares, almost 2 kilometres in circumference – Castelnaudary, through which huge quantities of wine and cereals were now going to transit, became the most important port on the canal between Toulouse and the Mediterranean, and experienced an unprecedented economic boom. "Downstreamers" enter the Grand Bassin after having passed successively beneath Pont-Neuf (13th century) and Vieux Pont, built during the development of the port in the 17th century. On the left, beautiful sailors' houses are lined up along the quayside. On the right, the island of Cybèle was created and planted with trees to protect the lake from gusts of wind, which drove ships on to the bank, and generated small storms capable of sinking vessels with even the heaviest loads. It was occupied for many years by a snack bar which has now disappeared.

The town and its surroundings are worth an extended stopover. In Castelnaudary itself, take time to stroll around the squares and streets, often lined with very handsome buildings, including some beautifully-crafted townhouses, and walk to Saint-Michel Collegiate Church (14th century) with its particularly remarkable Gothic and Renaissance porch-bell tower, the *Présidial* – former court of Sénéchaussée (16th and 17th century) – which houses an interesting archaeological museum, and Cugarel Mill (17th century) – as much for its viewpoint as for the quality of its restoration – the last survivor of the ten or so mills which, at the start of the century were still in operation in the town's upper reaches.

In the surrounding area, at least one site is worth a bicycle trip, since its distance from the canal makes it

Saint-Roch quadruple lock in Castelnaudary.

Cugarel windmill (17th century) on the upper reaches of Castelnaudary.

From the mill in Villeneuve-la-Comptal, near Castelnaudary, there is an outstanding view.

difficult to access on foot unless you have plenty of time: Villeneuve-la-Comptal (7 to 8 kilometre return trip) holds the ruins of a medieval fortress, a very beautiful church built in the 14th century, and a 17th century windmill.

Downstream from Castelnaudary, the hilly terrain forced the canal's builders to realise some genuine technical feats. To Bram, namely in the space of about fifteen kilometres, twelve locks succeed one another – of which one quadruple, one triple and one double – in order to compensate for an altitude difference of more than 46 metres, and there is also a large number of constructions: nine bridges, two aqueducts, two overflow channels and one spillway. Naturally, the reaches are very short: thus, just 418 metres separate Vivier and Guillermin Locks. This part of the route is going to be a lesson in slowness and we are going to learn that, on the canal, time does not pass at the same pace as elsewhere. No matter the number of kilometres totted up at the end of the day, you will quickly understand that what is important is the succession of small pleasures: negotiating the locks' entries and exits, using the handle to open and close the gates, admiring the perfection of the constructions designed by Riquet – the precision of the curves on the side walls, the rough beauty of a bollard carved out of stone, the charm of a lock house, the elegance of an aqueduct's arches – and chatting a while with the lock-keeper.

With its four chambers, Saint-Roch Lock, on the way out of the Grand Bassin, is one of the canal's major works. It was here that travellers coming from Toulouse with the "mail carriage" spent the first "*couchée*" (night stopover). Evidence of this is still visible in buildings such as the old hotel, the stables and the chapel. Unfortunately, the site has been spoiled by an unsightly flourmill built on the former site of the mills which used to take advantage of the powerful waterfall – 9.42 metres – between the two reaches. And, if the operator authorises it, do not hesitate to spend a few moments with him in the small tower from where he controls the locks: you will learn a great deal, including, and

The towpath has now become a playground for walkers and fishermen.

The lock-keepers

As with lighthouse keepers, there are those who have jobs to make you dream. Who would not like to spend a week or a month – why not a lifetime – in the quiet of the humble and delightful lock houses where they often live? Their official title is "operator" but, too bad, we will continue to call them by their more poetic title of lock-keeper. Without them, the huge hydraulic machine of the canal would not work, because their work goes far beyond opening and closing the gates and supervising the more or less approximate manoeuvres of amateur sailors: maintenance and repair of the locks, the banks and the constructions occupy them mainly when the canal is closed to navigation.
Meetings with lock-keepers set the pace of life on the canal. There are those who enjoy a laugh – almost all –, the grouches – very few –, the garrulous and the taciturn, the serious and the funny, those who paint, those who sculpt, those who have turned their lock into an annex of the Facteur Cheval's palace, or a miniature botanical garden. None of them leaves you indifferent, each one has something to say, on condition that you show the minimum of politeness by lending a hand or taking the time to chat.
Will they disappear one day? Is the increasing automation of locks a threat? Voies Navigables de France takes into account their fundamental role of coordination and reception now that, on many canals and rivers, tourism has replaced professional waterway transport. In all events, let us hope that lock-keepers – there are still sixty on the Canal du Midi – never join the large graveyard of forgotten professions because the canals will surely lose part of their spirit.

The "control tower" for Saint-Roch automatic lock, in Castelnaudary, with Henri Pelissier, the operator at the controls.

Some locks are veritable gourmet stopovers.

Proper use of the locks...

The Canal du Midi, the Canal Latéral à la Garonne, the Canal de Jonction and the Canal de la Robine are open to pleasure boating from the third Saturday in March to the first week in November. The rest of the year comprises a period of so-called "unemployment", during which major maintenance work is undertaken necessitating the draining of certain sections of the canal, and a period of "on demand" navigation during which individuals may use the canal on the condition of obtaining prior authorisation.
The locks are open from 8 am to 5.30 pm in March and November, from 8 am to 6 pm in October, from 8 am to 6.30 pm in April and September, from 8 am to 7 pm in May and from 8 am to 7.30 pm in June, July and August. The locks are closed from 12.30 pm to 1.30 pm.
On the Lot and the Baïse, navigation is authorised from April to October inclusive and the locks are open from 9 am to 7 pm.

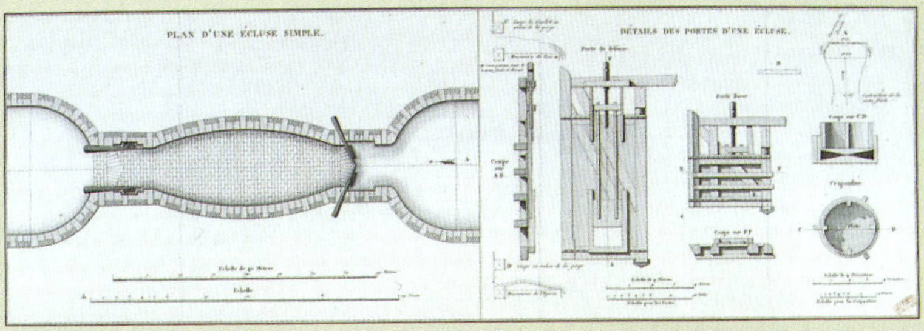

Plan of a single lock.
Toulouse, Paul-Dupuy Museum.
Inv. No. 67.31.10. Photo STC.

Cloister of the Benedictine abbey of Saint-Papoul. The 14th century sculpted capitals are particularly remarkable.

Polychrome wooden reliquary, Saint-Papoul Abbey.

above all, the errors not to commit as captain of a small barge.

After Saint-Roch, another stop can be made at Guerre Lock. The village of Saint-Martin-la-Lande is situated less than 1 kilometre away, which, apart from a gateway saved from the destruction of its ancient ramparts, has a superb Romanesque and Gothic church. However, above all, it is the proximity of Saint-Papoul which makes this stopover worthwhile. In a small isolated valley, 5 kilometres north of the canal, this Benedictine abbey is all the more worth the visit because, strangely, it is still largely ignored by tourists. However, it is regrettable that the village which houses it, where there are some very beautiful houses and the interesting remains of fortifications, has been particularly ill-treated by some extremely unsightly "modernisations". However, the cloister, with its twin-columned capitals sculpted with flowers and a remarkable bestiary, and the Cathedral – Saint-Papoul was the centre of the diocese from the 14th century – with a 12th century choir, narthex and apsidiole, are true gems of Occitan religious architecture.

Downstream from Guerre to Sainte-Eulalie Bridge (P.K. 89), the Canal passes through peaceful landscapes and pleasant, sleepy villages succeed one another along its banks – Pexiora, Villepinte, Bram, Alzonne – which, although they do not offer very many notable architectural treasures all provide an opportunity for an enjoyable walk. Along the way, take time to admire some beautiful constructions such as Tréboul aqueduct (a little upstream from the lock of the same name), built at the end of the 17th century by Vauban, Mezeran aqueduct (after P.K. 76), Rebenty aqueduct (between P.K. 83 and 84), the work of Riquet, and Espitalet aqueduct (upstream from P.K. 88). As you pass the port of Bram, you will recall that this small town – so ravaged over the centuries that, apart from the remains of its fortifications

The village of Sainte-Eulalie, dominated by the Romanesque bell tower of its parish church.

and a partially Gothic church, has preserved very few vestiges of its long history – was one of the birthplaces of the Cathar heresy before being laid siege to and taken by Simon de Montfort, who had the eyes put out and the tongues cut out of all its inhabitants. At Béteille Lock, it is still possible to see the old inn where "mail carriage" passengers coming from Toulouse were welcomed for their second *"dînée"* (lunch stop). And, we will take time to drop anchor for a while at P.K. 89 to visit Sainte-Eulalie (700 metres away), a very beautiful village with a remarkable *Maison Consulaire* (town hall) and a church with a Romanesque bell tower.

The Maison Presbytérale (12th century) in Villesèquelande.

Carcassonne is now only twelve kilometres and four locks away. However, do not be in too much of a hurry. Before the marvels of this fairytale town, you still have a few other treasures to discover. The canal, which winds its way through a series of short meanders, even appears to be inviting you to do so. Thus, at Villesèque Lock, you may complete a loop passing through Villesèquelande (800 metres away) – for its Romanesque-Gothic church and its 12th century *Maison Presbytérale* – Pezens (2 kilometres from Villesèquelande) – for its medieval streets and fortified church – and Caux (1.5 kilometres from the lock) – for its medieval and Renaissance castle, its 12th and 14th century church and its 16th century presbytery.

Further downstream, between P.K. 101 and 103, Foucaud overflow channel and Saume and Arnouze aqueducts are among the canal's most interesting constructions. With the consuls of Carcassonne initially refusing to participate in financing the canal, it was decided that it would

The walled town of Carcassonne: a medieval gem revisited by Viollet-le-Duc.

skirt the town to the north along the Fresquel valley. Although this error – demonstrated among other things by the economic boom in Castelnaudary – was very quickly and very bitterly regretted, more than a century was needed to correct it. In effect, it was only in 1810, after difficult and costly works – excavation of new reaches in the rock, construction of spillways, overflow channels and aqueducts – that the junction between the Ville Basse and the canal was finally completed. Thus, over about ten kilometres upstream and downstream of Carcassonne, the canal we follow is no longer the one designed by Riquet. Before entering the capital of Aude, we recommend two final visits, the first to Pennautier (about 2 kilometres from Douce Lock), a former fortified village where a very beautiful castle was built in the 17th century, and, near Foucaud overflow channel, a rare botanical garden, where more than 500 Mediterranean plant species flourish.

There is no need to tell you that Carcassonne (Ville Basse next to the port, the walled town less than 2 kilometres away) requires a long stopover. Almost everything has been seen and said about the almost unreal splendour of the walled town. It is true that, when restoring it, Viollet-le-Duc sometimes allowed his imagination to prevail over historical rigour. But, at least he saved the site from oblivion and, even better, in view of the general indifference of his contemporaries, from complete ruin. Temple merchants have tended to invade the streets and squares, insulting the old stones with their unsightly displays of

Tréboul Lock, near which Vauban had a superb aqueduct built.

pseudo antiques and trinkets barely worthy of a medieval form of Disneyland. But, it is the cost of fame. Nothing can touch it, not the grotesque miniature train which jolts its human cargo around the ramparts, or the piles of plastic armour and "I Love Carcassonne" T-shirts in the garish window displays: the magic of these towers and walkways, battlements and watchtowers, moats and drawbridges is so powerful that mercantile vulgarity barely skims its surface.

We will not go over what a visit to Carcassonne should involve: simply equip yourself with a good guidebook and comfortable walking shoes and enjoy a dreamy stroll along the streets and through the squares, along the ramparts and the Chemin des Lices. Of course, you will spend time at the Porte de l'Aude and the Porte de Narbonne, the Count's Castle and Saint-Nazaire-et-Saint-Celse Basilica, as well as the twenty-six towers accessible to walkers. Often neglected by tourists, who only have eyes for the walled town, the Ville Basse – a bastide built in the 13th century by Saint Louis – with its chequerboard

The port of Carcassonne, on the edge of the Ville Basse, a bastide built in the reign of Saint Louis.

The ramparts of the walled town of Carcassonne by night: a display of unequalled beauty.

This lock in Fresquel is part of a series of constructions dating from after Riquet's death. Designed to join Carcassonne canal to the Canal du Midi, it comprises three locks and one intermediate basin.

pavements, townhouses, 14th century Pont Vieux and its Gothic cathedral, offers considerable peaceful charm which you will enjoy all the more because it is far from the crowds and still inhabited by real people who lead real lives. In total, do not plan to spend fewer than 24 hours in Carcassonne, and be sure to arrive in the morning in order to obtain a place at the port which only has thirty, much sought after, berths.

Northeast of Carcassonne, the canal joins its old route at the canal bridge built in 1802 during works designed to prevent spates on the Fresquel, a particularly capricious river. Immediately downstream, Fresquel Locks – one double and one single – are separated by the shortest reach on the entire Two Seas system: only 250 metres. 1.5 kilometres from the second lock, from the upper reaches of Villemoustaussou, a circular village which preserves the ruins of its old fortress, there is a final, very beautiful view over the walled town of Carcassonne. Slightly further on –

A canal bridge enables the Canal du Midi to cross the unpredictable Fresquel mountain stream.

almost 4 kilometres – the beautiful village of Conques-sur-Orbiel offers an opportunity for a short excursion, as much for its medieval remains as for its Romanesque-Gothic church.

The canal, which now closely follows the course of the River Aude through a hilly landscape, curves around a large meander before reaching Trèbes. On the way, take a break at Villedubert Lock and visit Bouilhonac (2 kilometres away), a particularly picturesque site, which from its tumultuous past – it was ravaged during the Wars of Religion – has retained an interesting Romanesque church and the ruins of a fortress, and Malves-en-Minervois, famous for its 16th century castle, its Gothic church, and also the spectacular menhir not far from the Carcassonne entrance to the village.

Just before Trèbes (between P.K. 116 and 117), admire a magnificent canal bridge, representative of the improvements made to Riquet's work by Vauban. Originally, the Oriel, a mountain stream known for its violent spates, used to cross the canal along a simple roadway, which, every year, led to interruptions in traffic and major cleaning work. Built in 1688, the three-arched construction now crosses the Orbiel, thus removing one of the most problematic obstacles encountered by Riquet between Toulouse and the Mediterranean.

It is after flowing beneath a sumptuous alley of plane trees more than 1 kilometre long that the canal enters Trèbes, the site of the second day's "*couchée*" (night stopover) for the "mail carriage" from Toulouse. As for many other localities in the region, this very old small town, situated at the confluence of the Orbiel and the Aude, was ravaged during the Albigensian crusade and the Wars of Religion, before seeing the disappearance of almost all its fortifications during the Revolution. Nevertheless, it still has plenty of charm and some beautiful remnants from its past, in particular,

A magnificent row of hundred year old plane trees shades the towpath at the entrance to Trèbes.

The tall silhouette of the Gothic Saint-Étienne Church in Trèbes.

an impressive five-arched bridge spanning the River Aude, the oldest parts of which date back to Roman times, and a 12th and 13th century church which offers an astonishing rarity: 350 corbels painted with human and animal figures and geometric shapes. Trèbes was an important stage in the canal's construction: it was within its walls that, in 1673, the works of the "first enterprise" were completed, namely the slightly more than 110-kilometre section from Toulouse excavated within about six years. The realisation of the "second enterprise" – Trèbes-Mediterranean section – which we know Riquet never saw completed, came up against countless technical and financial difficulties, to such an extent that Colbert even thought for a time of abandoning the project. Although the part of the canal we have just covered to reach Trèbes was excavated with relative ease, the part we are now going to follow was, for Riquet, a time of doubt and, sometimes, even despair.

Castelnaudary Cassoulet according to Jean-Pierre Poggioli.

Cassoulet by Jean-Pierre Poggioli, Chef at La Belle Époque in Castelnaudary.

Ingredients (for 5 people)

1kg of dried beans (preferably white beans). 2 legs of goose confit. 1kg of fresh pork sausages. 1lb of chine of pork confit. 1 bone of country-style ham. White stock (meat stock). Salt, pepper, bouquet garni. 100g of garlic.

Preparation
(24 hours in advance if possible)

Sort the beans and soak them in cold water for 10 hours. Place them in a flat-bottomed pan and cover them with 3l of stock and add 15g of salt, 5g of white pepper, the bouquet garni, 100g of chopped garlic, the leg of ham. Bring to the boil and slow cook for 2 hours. Place some beans at the bottom of an earthenware cassolette, then add the sausage, chine and goose legs, ensuring that each piece of meat is cut into six pieces. Cover with the remaining beans.
Moisten with the cooking juices and brown in a warm oven for 4 hours.

Cassoulet

Carcassonne Cassoulet by Jean-Claude Rodriguez.

Nothing is more risky than talking about this crowning glory of food. The Hundred Years War only lasted a century. The armistice in the Cassoulet war has not yet been signed between Castelnaudary, Toulouse and Carcassonne. Which of these capitals of good food holds the key? It would be unwise to decide, so, instead, let us hide behind a few generalities: for Robert, Cassoulet is "a stew of fillets of goose, duck, pork or mutton with white beans", prepared and served in an earthenware "cassole". However, each town, whilst boasting ownership of the dish, has its own variants. Connoisseurs refuse to categorise them, quite simply evoking the Holy Trinity. The "Father" would be the Castelnaudary Cassoulet – the oldest and most rustic, mainly accompanied by pork – the "Son" from Carcassonne – to which partridge is sometimes added – and the "Holy Spirit" from Toulouse – enriched with sausage and breadcrumbs. However, it should be noted that with the dish dating from before the white bean – which you will recall was brought from America during the time of the Great Explorers – no doubt, this dish was made originally with broad beans. Having said that, "each has his own recipe", writes Jean-Claude Rodriguez, the Chef at Château Saint-Martin-Trencavel in Montredon, near Carcassonne. "For me, there are as many Cassoulets as there are cooks, and, of course, I would say that mine is the best there is!"

Cassoulet with fresh broad beans by Dominique Toulousy, Chef at Les Jardins de l'Opéra in Toulouse.

Ingredients (for 4 people)
1kg of fresh or frozen broad beans.
1 carrot. 1 onion. Thyme and laurel.
10 garlic cloves peeled and chopped.
200g of salted belly of pork cut into four cubes of 50g. 4 legs of duck confit.
4 pork rind sausages. 4 pieces of Toulouse sausage, each 100g. 100g of duck fat.
100g of fresh pork rind.
2l of duck stock.

Preparation
Shell and peel the broad beans. Blanch the pork belly and refresh it. Sweat the duck fat, with the finely diced carrot and onion in a cooking pot then add the pork rind and the blanched pork belly. Cover with the duck stock, add the bouquet garni and chopped garlic and leave to cook for about 1 hour.
During this time, brown the duck confit, Toulouse sausage and pork rind sausage in a frying pan Add, along with the broad beans, and slow cook for about 20 minutes. Check the seasoning and pour into an earthenware cassolette and cook in a very hot oven (Gas 7-8) for 15 minutes to obtain a golden top layer.
Serve when ready.

Toulouse Cassoulet by Dominique Toulousy.

From Trèbes to the Lagoon of Thau

For a long while the canal follows the course of the River Aude, which it will leave shortly before Port-la-Robine, then joins the River Orb for a short while at the foot of the acropolis in Béziers, before joining the River Hérault in the region of Agde. At Trèbes, the canal starts its final, slow descent towards the Mediterranean, from which it is still separated by about twenty locks and an altitude difference of almost 90 metres. Its route becomes extraordinarily capricious, its meanders – sometimes actual hairpin bends – increase in number, and, on its banks, the landscapes become increasingly bright, vineyards and olive trees start to appear, architectural treasures succeed one another – Ensérune, Béziers, Agde – and, shortly, the sound of cicadas can be heard. At no point in the construction of the canal was Riquet's ingenuity deployed with such daring. He knew that time was short, that his critics were on the lookout for the slightest error, therefore, he dared everything and succeeded at it all: the Malpas underground passage and the septuple lock in

Left page:
The canal near Capestang.

Castel
Tower, fort, ramparts
Ruins
Noteworthy buildings
Religious buildings
Noteworthy curiosity
Museum

A pleasure barge at Marseillette Lock.

Puichéric Church, rebuilt in the 19th century after being burnt down by the Black Prince.

Fonserannes are both masterpieces in the masterpiece which is the canal.

After the triple lock marking the exit of Trèbes, the canal cuts a path through the beautiful hilly countryside of the Aude valley. Here, the engineers encountered some very serious obstacles, sometimes being forced to blow up entire cliff faces to create a passage, and increased the number of constructions: on the 9-kilometre reach leading to Marseillette Lock, there are five bridges, two aqueducts, an overflow channel and a spillway. Take a break at Marseillette for the village itself, with the remnants of its old fortifications and a Chappe tower, but, above all, for the huge dried lake – 2,000 hectares – the draining of which started in the reign of Henri IV and continued until the start of the 19th century, and of which, today, there remains a spectacular grid of channels. If you take a little time, you may also head southwards to Capendu (2 kilometres away) – for its outstanding Romanesque chapel Saint-Martin – and Barbaira (5 kilometres away) – for the charm of its medieval streets and its 13th and 14th century church – or northwards, to Badens (3.5 kilometres away) for the remains of its fortress and its Gothic church. At Fonfile triple lock, after Marseillette Lock, it is not uncommon to have to wait because of traffic, offering an opportunity to take a look at the exceptional church in Saint-Étienne de Blomac (about 1.5 kilometres away).

Roquecourbe-Minervois offers up its superb architecture in the heart of the vineyards of Aude.

Two reaches and 3 kilometres further on, whether you have been warned or not, you will inevitably spend a while at Aiguille Lock. How is it possible not to be fascinated by the humour and inventiveness of the animated sculptures with which the lock-keeper has covered the banks and quaysides of his small estate? In all cases, this eloquent and charming poet has turned his lock into one of the most unexpected sites on the canal. Nearby, do not miss a visit to the village of Puichéric (1 kilometre away), which, alongside some very beautiful houses, preserves a superb castle surrounded by ramparts and an interesting Gothic church. Slightly further on (1.5 kilometres from Puichéric), in the middle of the vineyards, Roquecourbe-Minervois is worth the detour for its castle and its 15th century castle chapel. After this, it is in La Redorte, where the canal follows two sharp meanders, that, other than the castle which dominates the village, the site of the "*dînée*" (lunch stop) on the third day, you will be able to admire the constructions in Argentdouble, which are among the most beautiful on the canal. The first we encounter, about 1 kilometre

The keep in Escales (11th century).

Saint-Martin-des-Tours Church in Escales. Its construction dates from the 10th century.

Until the end of the 19th century, the port of Homps was one of the most important on the canal.

downstream from La Redorte, is an extremely elegant fifty-metre long overflow channel with eleven arches built by Vauban in 1693. The second is an aqueduct, which provides a passage over the Torrent de l'Argentdouble, a tributary of the Aude with some devastating spates, built after Riquet's death in around 1688 to replace a simple roadway.

Downstream from Argentdouble, you will pass successively Jouarrès Lock and aqueduct before reaching the port of Homps, which, for three centuries, was one of the most important on the canal. Although the town, a former base for the Knights of Malta, was sacked on several occasions, in particular during the Albigensian crusade and the Wars of

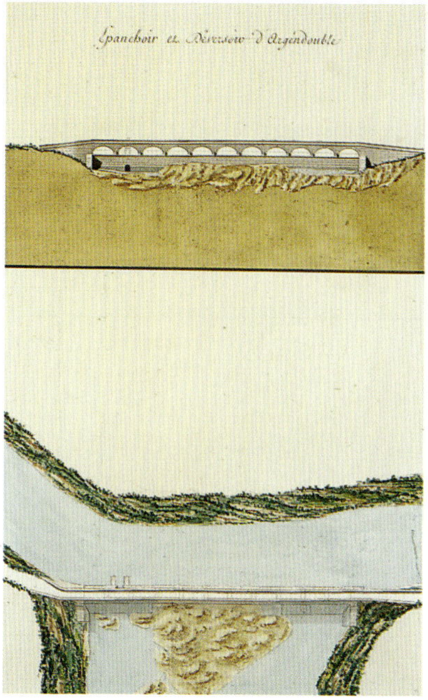

Argentdouble overflow channel.
VNF - South-western Regional Department - Canaux du Midi Archives. Photo Jean-Luc Auriol.

Right:
Argentdouble overflow channel, built after Riquet's death following plans by Vauban.

Religion, nevertheless, it has preserved a tower from its old castle and, above all, a very beautiful Romanesque chapel. About 3 kilometres away, the village of Tourouzelle is worth a short excursion, as much for its delightful setting as for the untouched beauty of its medieval streets.

Downstream from Homps, the canal continues to follow the course of the River Aude closely, sometimes, with no more than ten metres separating them. The hilly terrain required some major construction works, thus, in under 4 kilometres, you will encounter two double locks, four bridges and, above all, three canal bridges – Ognon, Bassane and Pechlaurier – built after Riquet's death to replace the roadways which regularly used to silt up the canal. After Pechlaurier Lock, do not miss a stop at Argens-Minervois, which, with the superb silhouette of its 14th century castle – sadly, poorly maintained – undoubtedly constitutes one of the most photogenic stages on the route. On the way out of the village, Argens Lock is the busiest on the canal with 11,000 boats a year, but, above all, it is the entrance to the longest reach – 53.490 kilometres – on the entire Two Seas canal. Until Béziers and the majestic water ladder in Fonserannes, there will be no more locks, but, you will be able to admire some of the most daring constructions ever designed by Riquet. It is possible to cover this reach in less than a day whilst also complying with navigation regulations, but, what a pity: there is so much to see that, on the contrary, it would be best to take the time to enjoy a slow cruise.

Although it is not possible to stop in all the villages along the canal, we should stop, at least for a short while and visit the most picturesque ones with the most history.

The village of Argens-en-Minervois and the huge towers of its 14th century castle.

Plaque in tribute to Riquet on Répudre canal bridge.

This is the case of Paraza, slightly off the route (3 kilometres away), which nestles at the foot of its 17th century castle and Sainte-Valière, a medieval village dominated by a belfry and the remains of its ancient fortress, which has a very beautiful Romanesque-Gothic church. Downstream from Paraza, less than 1 kilometre away, in the sharp bend of a hairpin meander, stands one of the canal's most astonishing constructions. To the stupefaction of his contemporaries, here, in order to cross the bed of the Répudre, a particularly unpredictable and violent mountain stream, Riquet dared to build what may well have been the very first canal bridge in the world. This invention marked a turning point: Vauban largely used the concept during his improvement works after Riquet's death, followed by all other subsequent canal builders.

Répudre canal bridge, Riquet's masterpiece, said to be the oldest in the world.

The old bookshop in Somail, one of the canal's attractions.

Seven kilometres after Répudre canal bridge, Le Somail is one of the most delightful stopovers on the reach. With its hump-backed bridge, its chapel and its ancient hostelry, this small village no doubt looks as it did three centuries ago, when it was the site of the "*couchée*" on the third day. Today's navigators continue to respect tradition, all the more willingly since the terraces of the gourmet inns which line the quayside and the curiosities of the old bookshop and its strange Hat Museum offer some irresistible attractions.

It is slightly over 2 kilometres from Somail, just downstream from Port-la-Robine – where nothing incites you

Somail port, the site of the "couchée" on the third day, pursues its ancient tradition with its inns and restaurants.

A peaceful stopover... On the canal, time seems to pass more slowly than elsewhere.

to dally other than material necessities such as water and fuel – that the link to the Canal de Jonction, excavated in 1787 to connect the Canal du Midi and the Canal de la Robine, can be found. Two superb constructions precede it: first of all Patiasses overflow channel, a wall crossed through by vaults which, with the help of an underflow gate, evacuate flood water to the bed of the Cesse; then the Cesse canal bridge, built after Riquet's death and which, standing 20 metres tall and 63 metres wide, is one of the largest on the canal.

From Cesse to Béziers, the canal appears to hesitate about the route to follow, firstly veering northwards in

The pure and simple beauty of the bridge in Argeliers.

a straight line – this section, slightly longer than 2.5 kilometres, excavated out of very hard rock was very difficult to realise – then changing its mind to head east and then south, before continuing towards the Mediterranean, multiplying the number of curves, meanders and sharp bends, as if it were trying to extend the unusual length of the *Grand Bief* (Long Reach) and leave time for navigators to enjoy the beauty of the landscapes they are passing through and take a break at some outstanding sites.

Thus, we will not fail to drop anchor at the port of Argeliers, a medieval village which, apart from the charm of its streets, offers some interesting remains of its ramparts and its fortress and an impressive fortified church. Six kilometres further on, just downstream from P.K. 178, you will notice an attractive collection of buildings, dating from the same period as the canal, comprising Pigasse Bridge and some old houses on the left bank. From there, religious art lovers, will not hesitate to travel the 4 kilometres to Quarante, where the beautiful 11th and 12th century Sainte-Marie Church can be found, home to a wealth of furnishings and treasures – sarcophagus, reliquary and shrines.

After Pigasse Bridge, the canal's route becomes more erratic and the number of aqueducts increases – there are seven within 8 kilometres, including Quarante aqueduct (upstream from P.K. 179), built by Vauban in 1693 – saying a great deal about the difficulties presented by the terrain. Downstream from Capestang – a superb small town dominated by the Gothic collegiate of Saint-Étienne and the castle of the Archbishops of Narbonne – a section

The tall silhouette of Saint-Étienne collegiate indicates the village of Capestang in the distance.

Without this tunnel, no doubt, the canal would never have been completed.

of the canal was even built overhanging the plain, which at that time was a true technical feat, although not one without risk since, in 1744, downstream from Poilhès, a 300 metre stretch of the canal was destroyed by a landslide. Also, it was very near here that Riquet was going to encounter one of the most challenging obstacles he ever had to overcome, the Colline de Malpas, which, standing perpendicular to the

The Maison du Malpas

Situated on the Malpas hill, a site laden with history in the heart of a region which has just as much to offer, the Maison du Malpas is the cultural and tourism centre for the *Communauté de communes "La Domitienne"*. The Maison du Malpas offers visitors an information point for details about tourism activities in the region, an exhibition centre, a multimedia space, a documentation centre and guided tours. The car park is the departure point for walks to the Lagoon of Montady, the oppidum of Ensérune or the Canal du Midi.

Centre touristique et culturel
La Maison du Malpas - Route de l'Oppidum - 34440 Colombiers
Tél. 04 67 32 88 77

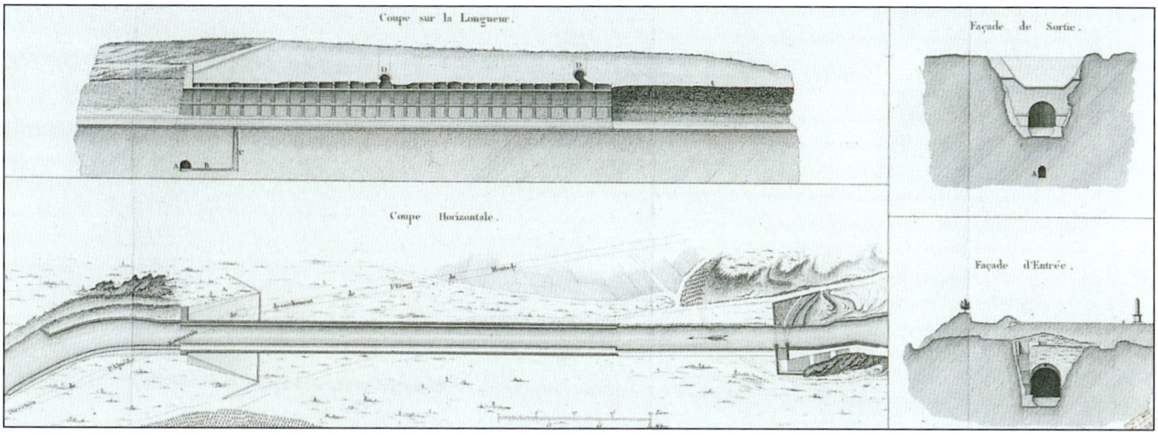

Vaulted roof of Malpas tunnel
Toulouse, Paul-Dupuy Museum.
Inv. No. 67.11.18. Photo STC.

intended route, appeared to be impassable. Pressed by time, crippled by debt and not wanting to create a long and costly diversion, he decided to dig a tunnel. However, initial excavation works revealed subsoil so friable that Colbert, charitably informed by Riquet's enemies of the dangers which this construction would present if it were completed, had the works stopped. But, Riquet was going to show the extent of his determination: pretending to comply with the request, he assembled a team which he charged with continuing the work in secret. They had to be quick, because the situation was becoming increasingly complex and, it was within the barely believable time of one week that the hill was crossed by a 165-metre long tunnel, the vault of which rises 8 metres above water level, consolidated by a series of supporting arches, which proved to be perfectly safe. Colbert bowed to this *fait accompli* and the triumphant Riquet was applauded by all. He had just opened the first navigation tunnel in the world and, what was even more important to him was

In the region of Poilhès, the terrain's difficulties necessitated huge works.

Ensérune oppidum, one of the major archaeological sites in the south of France.

the fact that he had won the right to continue his work.

A few hundred metres from Malpas tunnel, Ensérune oppidum, which dominates the canal and the plain of Beziers from its 100-metre high rocky outcrop, is one of the main archaeological sites in Languedoc. Excavations have revealed remarkably well-preserved remains of the civilisations which have succeeded each other here over seven centuries,

The old lake in Montady, which was drained in the Middle Ages, with its cartwheel-shaped drainage channels.

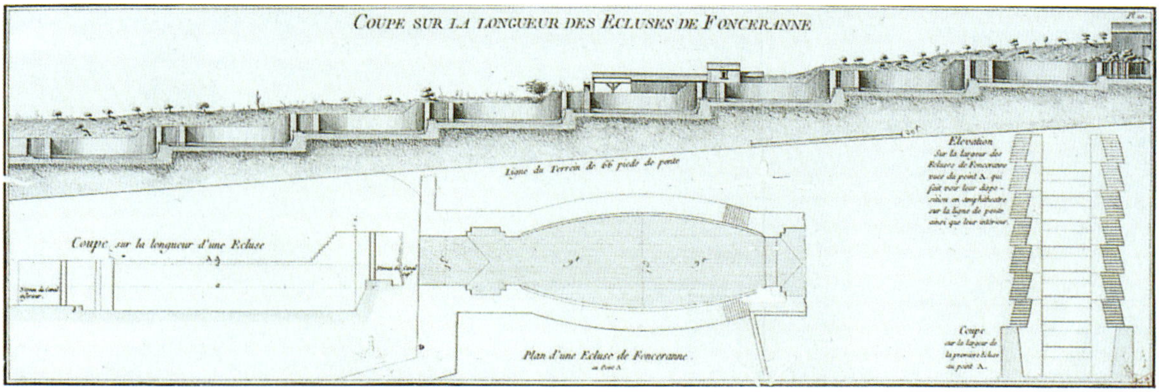

Section of Fonserannes Lock.
Toulouse, Paul-Dupuy Museum.
Inv. No. 67.38.10. Photo STC.

Iberian, Greek, Gaulish and Roman. Apparently destroyed several times, once in 3BC by Hannibal, before experiencing real prosperity under the Roman occupation, the oppidum was occupied until 1AD when the "Pax Romana", encouraging the populations of Narbonne to abandon their defensive sites, led to its being abandoned definitively.

From the promontory's summit, the view takes in a superb panorama stretching from the Cevennes to the sea. Below, to the north, is the unusual geometry of the ancient lake in Montady which was drained in the middle of the 13th century. Almost perfectly circular, it is divided into plots by drainage channels extending from the circumference to the centre giving it the appearance of a huge cartwheel laid out on the plain.

When leaving the oppidum, it would be a pity not to visit Nissan-lès-Ensérune, which has a remarkable Gothic church (14th century) and an interesting small archaeology and religious art museum.

The end of the *Grand Bief* (Long Reach) is now close. Its last meanders form a slow approach to Fonserannes "ladder", the astonishing masterpiece on a level with Répudre canal bridge and Malpas tunnel in terms of innovation, which Riquet bequeathed to his town of birth. In effect a sizeable obstacle lay at the entrance to Béziers: the need to overcome an altitude difference of almost 25 metres within the space of a few hundred metres, in order to reach the course of the River Orb, which skirts the

Fronserannes Locks.
(© VNF. P)

Fonserannes ladder: despite some modifications, one of Riquet's most daring constructions has lost none of its majestic beauty.

town to the south. For this, Riquet designed an enormous water ladder with eight steps, meaning eight locks, to compensate for the difference in height. Boats coming from Toulouse descended the ladder step by step and then followed the Orb for a short distance – the water level of which was regulated by a dam – before returning to the canal on the opposite bank, with those coming from the sea, naturally, completing the operation in reverse. It is true, that a few multiple locks did already exist, but, owing to its size, Fonserannes ladder was a worldwide "first" which amazed Riquet's contemporaries and which, today still, astonishes many by its conceptual audacity. Short as it may be, the passage along the Orb, with its frequent and unpredictable mood changes, presented a real danger, sometimes forcing traffic to be suspended. However, two centuries were needed before the decision was taken to build a canal bridge, which, apart from modifying the original route, led to the closure of the inferior lock and the downgrading of the reach preceding it, the "canalet" de Notre-Dame. Inaugurated in 1857, the Orb canal bridge, admirably elegant with its multiple arches and dressed stone facing, is a tribute to Riquet's successors. More so, on all counts, than the electric traction "water slope" built in 1983, which was supposed, if not to completely replace the seven locks, at least to offer a faster passage – 6 minutes instead of 40 – but, the operation of which, at present, is limited temporarily by overhead costs and the need for greater reliability.

Without a doubt, Béziers is much less lively than Toulouse and less magical than Carcassonne. But it is beautiful – discovering, beyond the arches of Pont Vieux reflected in the River Orb, the tall silhouette of the cathedral dominating the acropolis is always dazzling – and appears to be a model of a gentle way of life – which does not exclude a violent and very southern passion for rugby, bull-fighting and wine! – where, it is always a pleasure to spend a little time. However, the town's history is

Béziers. The canal bridge.

very turbulent and often tragic. During the Albigensian crusade, after the town's Catholics refused to hand over the Cathars, the crusaders proceeded with a terrible massacre to the cry of "Kill them all, God will recognise his own". Despite the sieges, fires and pillaging, it has retained many architectural treasures. Do not miss a stroll through its

The 240-metre Béziers canal bridge, built in the 19th century, is the longest on the canal.

Saint-Nazaire cathedral and the old town of Béziers seen from the banks of the River Orb.

Statue of Paul Riquet in Béziers.

old neighbourhoods, a visit to Saint-Nazaire Cathedral, Sainte-Aphrodise Basilica, the churches of La Madeleine and Saint-Jacques, the view from the Jardin des Évêques, a moment of dreaming in the coppices on the Plateau des Poètes, and, of course, a meal at one of the terraces along the Allées Pierre-Paul-Riquet, where the heart of the town beats by day and by night. Because Béziers has shown its gratitude to its most ingenious child by giving his name to this magnificent promenade – vaguely reminiscent of the "ramblas" in Barcelona – and erecting a statue in his honour.

Downstream from Béziers, and for the thirty remaining kilometres to the Lagoon of Thau, the canal cuts a path through the low plains which line the Mediterranean, even approaching the coast to within 1,200 metres. Its route becomes less erratic and its meanders are fewer in number as if it were now in a hurry to reach the end. But, this does not mean that nature has stopped putting obstacles in its path. Here, Riquet had to call upon all his imagination's resources to solve the problem of crossing the Libron (P.K. 225). This modest waterway, subject to violent spates, could not be crossed by an aqueduct because the level of the canal above water – about 2 metres – was now too low. The solution found was extremely ingenious: when low in water, the Libron flowed along a channel built below the canal on each side of which two walls were built. In the event of a spate, a single-deck barge was sunk between these two walls, at right angles to the stream, the waters of which now crossed the canal over the two walls and the deck of the barge. The system which can be seen today dates from 1855, and whilst it uses the same principle – creating an artificial bed for the floodwaters of the Libron over the canal – allows uninterrupted traffic: a system com-

The Libron system, the ingenuity of which still inspires admiration today.

prising two sets of mobile boxes forms a sort of roof which becomes the new bed for the Libron. These two "covers" may be deployed separately using sluice gates which direct the flow either towards one – the second being stored away – then towards the other – the first, in turn, being folded away – thus enabling the boat to move as if from one chamber to the other.

Between Béziers and the Lagoon of Thau, there are a few essential stopovers, firstly in Villeneuve-lès-Béziers, for its picturesque streets and the fortified bell tower (10th – 14th century) of Saint Etienne Church, and then in Portiragnes and Vias for their "black churches", typical of the region's architecture, and, finally, and above all, in Agde, with this town founded twenty-five

Vias Church built in black lava rock abundant in the region.

The banks of the River Hérault in Agde, a town touched by grace and bathed in the light of the Mediterranean.

centuries ago by Phoenician Greeks offering so many architectural treasures. Before the alluvium carried by the River Rhone modified the shape of the coast – its ancient port is now 4 kilometres from the sea – and competition from Montpellier, Aigues-Mortes and Sète ruined it, it was, for many long years, one of the most prosperous towns in the western Mediterranean. As if unable to forget its glorious past, Agde appears to be shrouded in mourning. But, the "black pearl of Languedoc" may very well be dressed in dark colours – it is built in ash-coloured volcanic rock – but it, nevertheless, continues to be astonishingly bright

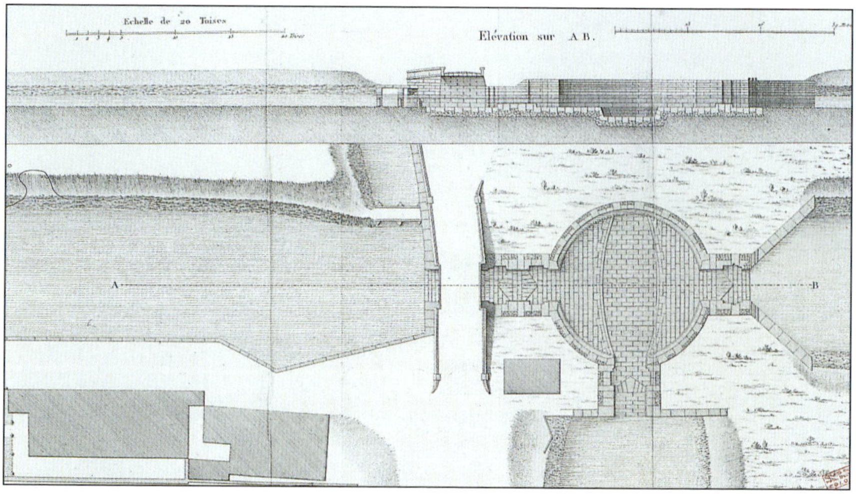

Plan and section of Agde Lock.
Toulouse, Paul-Dupuy Museum.
Inv. No. 67.31.13. Photo STC.

Unique of its kind, Agde round lock.

and gay. In its unpredictable streets and its flower-covered squares, on its cheerful quaysides, where crooked houses are reflected in the waters of the River Hérault, in the area around Saint-Étienne Cathedral with its severe harmony, everything is wreathed in grace, in the image of the bronze Ephebos delivered from the mud of the river in 1964, coveted by all the museums of the world, but from which the town has never separated itself and which, today, has become its emblem. And, with beauty calling beauty, it is not by chance that Riquet designed for Agde a construction unique of its kind, the famous "round lock", the outline of which, sadly, was damaged by some ill-advised modernisation works, but which is still one of the most remarkable on the canal.

Downstream from Agde, the smell of the sea and the flight of pink flamingos announce the end of a long journey. Another two locks and, after a final meander, Les Onglous lighthouse appears marking the arrival in the Lagoon of Thau with the upper reaches of Sète in the distance, where the work of Pierre-Paul Riquet comes to an end in great style.

Les Onglous lighthouse marks the arrival in the Lagoon of Thau.

The port of Les Onglous where boats sometimes have to shelter when the mistral blows on the Lagoon of Thau.

Bouzigues oysters.

The Lagoon of Thau

It is definitely the largest – 8,000 hectares – on the coast of Languedoc, but, after all, it is merely a lagoon.

And, yet... The passengers on the "mail carriage", who, after a four-day trip, saw Les Onglous lighthouse, could almost believe that they had arrived in Sète, but that was without counting on the anger of the mistral wind, which, sometimes, forced them to spend several days sheltering on the canal. It was necessary to wait until the middle of the 19th century and the introduction of a steam boat service for the crossing of the lake to be possible in all weather conditions. Today still, the greatest care is advised for navigators, who are not authorised to take to the water when the wind exceeds 26 knots.

Separated from the Mediterranean by a thin 20-kilometre long stretch of coast, the Lagoon of Thau is actually a small inland sea with its own beaches, ports - Balaruc-les-Bains, Bouzigues, Marseillan, Mèze – fleet and fishermen. Since Antiquity, the inhabitants of its shores have drawn a large part of their income from shellfish farming. The Romans were great enthusiasts of the flat oysters growing wild there. But, over the years, the fragile environment led to numerous epidemics – the last in 1971 – which caused the disappearance of the indigenous

The Noilly-Prat open-air storehouse.

oysters. Those sold today under the name of "Bouzigues" are hollow oysters from a very resistant Japanese strain. They are farmed using a special technique – suspended on growing tables – suited to the absence of tides: immersed 24 hours a day, they reach maturity within 12 to 20 months, namely one year ahead of the Atlantic or Channel oysters.

The small coastal towns have plenty of charm. Do not miss a visit to Balaruc-les-Bains for the remains of its 3rd century basilica and its 18th century Pavillon Sévigné – Balaruc-le-Vieux for its superb site on a rocky outcrop and its 14th century church – Bouzigues for its Museum of the Lagoon – Mèze for its Gothic church – and, above all, Marseillan, the most delightful port on the lake, home to the very unusual Noilly-Prat storehouse where in the thousands of oak casks laid out in the open between the walls of a huge enclosed courtyard, the famous aperitif drink finishes maturing.

La Pointe-Courte fishing village in Sète.

Marseillan port, one of the most charming on the Lagoon of Thau.

The quayside of the Canal Royal in Sète. New town desired by Riquet who made it his "third enterprise", it was built to serve as a Mediterranean outlet for the Canal du Midi.

Sète

Where does its infinite attraction come from? Compared to its beautiful neighbours and rivals, Agde and Aigues-Mortes, Sète does not offer prestige, a long history, or the splendour of outstanding monuments. In a region where the smallest village is able to lay claim to a several thousand year history, the "Venice of Languedoc" built from 1666 onwards, is a new town. It is true that evidence has been found on its site of the existence of Gallo-Roman occupation and a medieval settlement.

But, of a town, nothing. It is to the gradual silting over of Agde, Aigues-Mortes and Narbonne, the desire of Colbert to equip France with a powerful Mediterranean port, and that of Riquet to offer an outlet for the Canal du Midi – it was his "third enterprise" – that Sète owes its existence. Perhaps that is its secret: as the youngest port town in Languedoc, it has all the colours, gaiety and freshness of youth.

In Sète do not look for amazing churches or magnificent townhouses. Its assets are elsewhere. In its aromas of the sea and the garrigue, in its light, in the celebratory atmosphere of its quaysides, in the incredible beauty of the views from the top of Mont Saint-Clair, in the poignant charm of the fishermen's cemetery where Paul Valéry and Georges Brassens are buried.

It is not surprising. If Sète is a town of poets, it is because the town itself is a town of poems.

Sète. The Railway swing bridge.

Paul Valéry's tomb in the fishermen's cemetery in Sète.

LY 7915

From the Canal du Midi to the canals of the Midi

Although it is indisputable that Riquet's ambition – to connect the Atlantic to the Mediterranean by waterway – had been a crowning success, it is also true that the Canal du Midi was far from resolving all the problems of traffic. In Toulouse, the need to follow the Garonne to reach the Gironde and Bordeaux implied a load transfer, with the canal's barges being unable to navigate on this fast and dangerous river, on which, furthermore, navigation was often interrupted. The

Escudies Lock on the Minor Canal of the Garonne.

Port-la-Nouvelle, sea outlet of the Canal de la Robine.

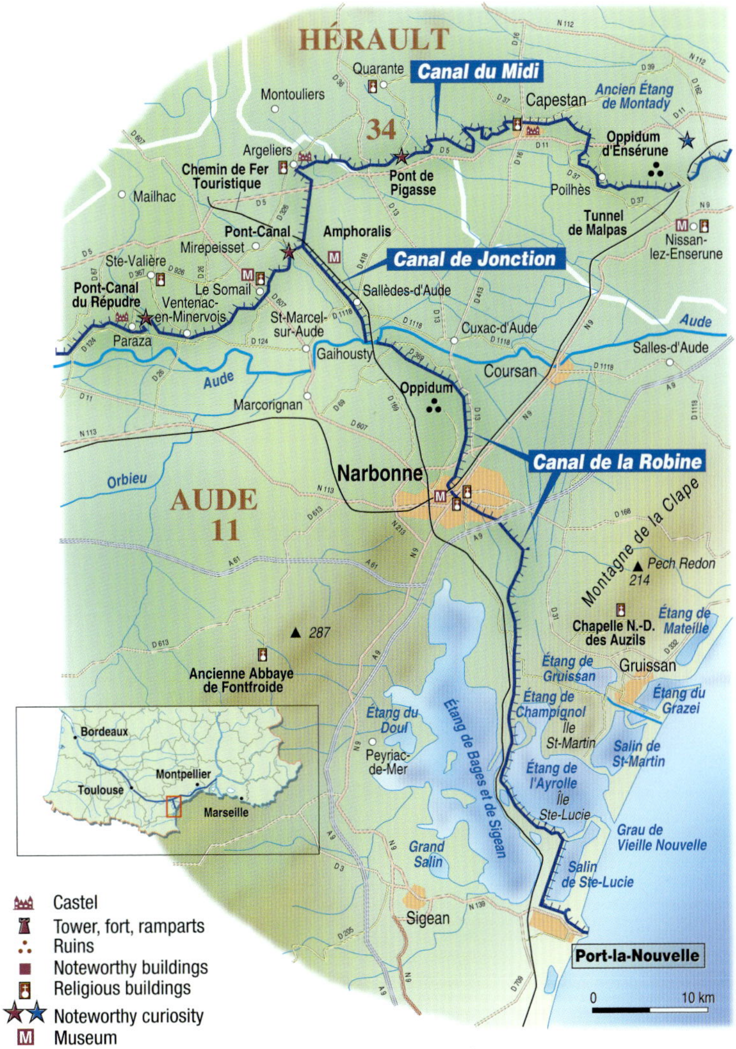

Left page:
Entrance of the canal du Rhône à Sète near the Lagoon of Ingril.

Barges on the Canal de la Robine in Narbonne.

same type of problem continued to be posed in the Mediterranean: from the River Rhone, the royal route of river trade between Southern and Northern Europe, to Sète, the entry point to the canal, it was necessary to use a maritime link and, in consequence, put up with lost time and the cost of a double load transfer. Finally, the preference given to the Béziers-Agde-Sète route had left out Narbonne, depriving the canal of the excellent sea outlet of Port-la-Nouvelle. Both Riquet and Vauban had taken these problems into account, but after the huge human and financial efforts which the creation of the Canal du Midi alone demanded, there was no question of launching the construction of new manmade waterways, especially since their profitability was uncertain. It was necessary to wait almost two centuries after Riquet's death for the successive opening of the Canal de Jonction, the Canal de la Robine, the Canal du Rhône à Sète and the Canal Latéral à la Garonne and the final completion of the junction between the Two Seas.

The Canal de Jonction and the Canal de la Robine

Riquet's preference for the Béziers-Agde-Sète route was a true disaster for Narbonne, even more difficult to accept by its inhabitants since the town already had a very solid tradition in manmade waterways. In effect, in Roman times, an initial canal had been built as far as the sea through the Lagoon of Sigean, enabling Narbonne to become one of the major ports on the Mediterranean. In the Middle Ages, the River Aude changed its course passing around the town instead of through it, thus forcing the inhabitants of

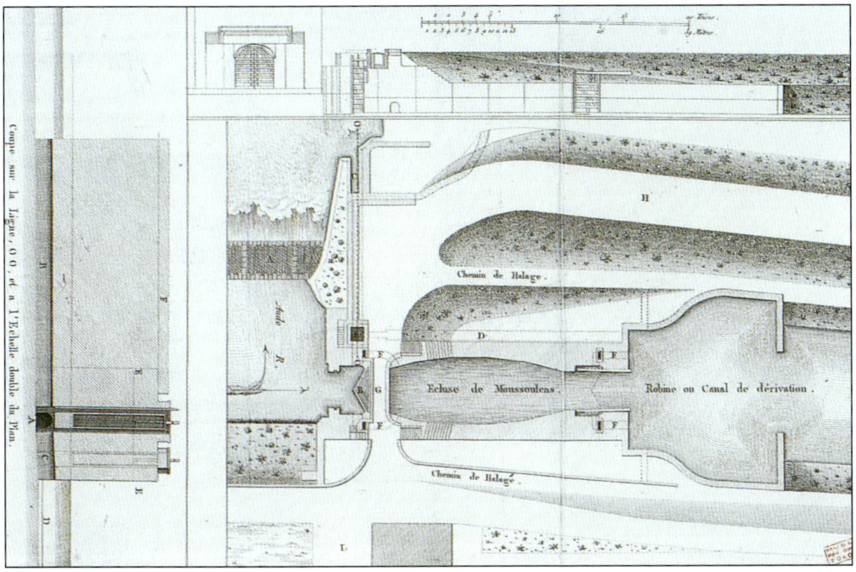

Plan and section of Moussoulens Lock.
Toulouse, Paul-Dupuy Museum. Inv. No. 67.31.15. Photo STC.

Cesse lock on the Canal de Jonction.

Narbonne to dig a channel from Gailhousty in order to ensure their supply of drinking water. This channel was later enlarged to make it navigable. Thus, the Canal de la Robine, along with the old Roman canal, formed a coherent and viable ensemble which only needed a 5-kilometre extension to join it to the Canal du Midi. No one doubts that Riquet, given the time and money, would have built this junction. After Riquet's death, Vauban initiated the work but came up against the hostility of the town councillors of Béziers and Sète and, above all, the refusal of Riquet's heirs – the canal's owners, let us not forget – unwilling to commit to large expenses while they were still struggling to pay back their father's debts. Finally, at long last, in 1787 the Canal de Jonction was built as far as the Canal de la Robine, and Narbonne, now open to the outside world, although unable to rediscover its ancient role as a maritime port, was able, at least, to become an important link in the Two Seas Canal.

Gailhousty overflow channel, without doubt the most attractive construction on the Canal de la Robine.

The vineyard of Saint-Marcel-d'Aude.

From the junction with the Canal du Midi to Port-la-Nouvelle in slightly less than 36 kilometres and thirteen locks, the Canal de Jonction and the Canal de la Robine offer the opportunity for a superb and relatively short cruise – three to four days are needed for the return trip. First of all, there is the long straight line of the Canal de Jonction, the royal waterway shaded by a double row of stone pines, which leads to Sallèles-d'Aude, a delightful small town which, from 4AD, was a centre for wine-making, as can be seen by the amphora produced in almost industrial quantities in the surrounding area, now exhibited at the Amphoralis Museum less than 2 kilometres away – then to Gailhousty, where, near a monumental overflow channel built in about 1780, we cross the River Aude to enter the Canal de la Robine. Only one reach remains – less than 4.5 kilometres – before Gua Lock, the entrance to Narbonne. It would be difficult to imagine a more

Ancient maritime port, Narbonne had to wait until the end of the 18th century to be joined to the Canal du Midi by the Canal de Jonction and the Canal de la Robine.

beautiful arrival in a town. After the canal has flowed through the vaulted canopy of plane trees along the quaysides, and darkened briefly below the medieval Pont des Marchands – one of the last in France which has retained its old houses – Narbonne appears before you in all its splendour: the incomplete Cathedral of Saint-Just, Saint-Paul Basilica, the Archbishops' Palace and the aristocratic houses which line its paved streets form an urban landscape of unforgettable perfection. At that point, you may, of course, choose to turn back. But, downstream from Narbonne, in a landscape of wide-open skies, the Robine offers a journey of strange and moving poetry along the thin strip of Sainte-Lucie Island, between lagoons and lakes, to the accompaniment of the flight of wildfowl and the smell of the sea, through these harsh and almost inhuman landscapes occasionally encountered on the shores of the Mediterranean. And, you will not regret having gone as far as Port-la-Nouvelle – a sort of town at the end of the world – one of the largest ports in France – today, ranked seventh – accessible to "freshwater sailors".

In Narbonne, the Archbishops' Palace (above) and Saint-Just-et-Saint-Pasteur Basilica (opposite) form an outstanding religious, civil and military ensemble.

The Cistercian abbey of Fontfroide is one of the most beautiful in France. The Louis XIV courtyard is surrounded by 13th century buildings, one of which was embellished with a classic-style fronton in the 17th century.

Fontfroide Abbey

It is situated rather far from the Canal de la Robine, but it is of such outstanding beauty that it would be a pity not to devote an excursion to it. About fifteen kilometres from Narbonne, Fontfroide Abbey nestles at the end of a valley in the Corbières hills, in a stark landscape of garrigue and ochre-coloured sandstone, softened slightly by the rounded shapes of the vineyards and the Tuscany-style silhouettes of cypress trees. Founded in 1093, it was part of the Cistercian order until the middle of the 12th century, a period of exceptional prosperity for it. One of its Abbots, Jacques Fournier, even became Pope in 1334 under the name of Benoît XII. But, in 1348, the Black Death struck carrying away three quarters of its monks and the abbey never recovered. Held in commendam in the middle of the 15th century, it saw a succession of abbots who, more attracted by its wealth than by the rigours of monastic life, turned some of its buildings into genuine palaces. At the Revolution, its property was divided up, but, by chance, was not irreparably damaged. In 1858, a Cistercian community from Sénanque reoccupied it, but the resurrection did not last long with the promulgation of the law against religious congregations in 1901 forcing the monks into exile. Auctioned in 1908, it was acquired by a rich art-loving winemaker who saved it from ruin and carried out exemplary restoration work.

It is thanks to this patron that Fontfroide has been restored to us today in its full glory, with its magnificently stark 12th century abbatial church, its 12th and 14th century cloister with its wonderful sculpted capitals, its huge monks' dormitory and its sumptuous abbatial dwelling house.

The cloister dates mainly from the 12th century.

The vaults with an incredible span.

The Canal du Rhône à Sète: vast horizons.

The Canal du Rhône à Sète

It was only in 1808 that the canal providing the junction between the River Rhone and the Lagoon of Thau was completed. How is it possible not to be amazed? Its economic importance was obvious, the distance – less than 100 kilometres – was not great, and the terrain's configuration – a series of low plains, numerous lagoons and rivers ensuring a constant supply of water – did not present any major obstacles. It is true that at the end of the 17th century, a waterway was excavated between Sète and Aigues-Mortes. But, the work was not continued and the original idea is all the more difficult to understand in the case of Aigues-Mortes, which the gradual silting of the coast had now relocated in the hinterland, being already no more than a dead-end. It was necessary to wait until the First Empire for the project to be relaunched and, this time, completed within the space of a few years. The Southwest of France was now able to increase its river traffic with the River Rhone, which, via the River Saône, communicates with the huge navigable river and canal network of Northern and Eastern Europe.

From Sète to Beaucaire – 97 kilometres, 22 bridges and 3 locks – the canal passes through some astonishing water landscapes. It flows along a series of lagoons – from Frontignan to La Grande-Motte no fewer than ten in under 60 kilometres – either along narrow strips of sand, or through the lagoons themselves without its powerful waters ever being combined with theirs thanks to the canal's high banks. Then, after Aigues-Mortes, we

The solitude of spaces without limits, the superb severity of the landscapes, the world of the Canal du Rhône à Sète is one of incomparable outlandishness.

discover the melancholic horizons of the marshes, rice paddies and flooded prairies of the Petite Camargue, before gradually, the land dries between Saint-Gilles and Beaucaire and, in the distance, the outline of the hills of the Gard appears.

Paradoxically, there is nothing tedious about this slow journey through the huge rectilinear landscapes which line the canal: the flight of pink flamingos, galloping horses crazed by freedom, the mineral immobility of black-coated bulls, the wind blowing through the reeds. We sail through a different world, through ever-repeated landscapes, but which always appear to be different, where distances and time no longer exist. And, in the same way as a well-travelled sailor, each port of call is like arriving on a new island.

Some of these ports of call should be avoided. Although, in former times, the concreting of the coastline did meet obvious social needs and although the architecture of Palavas-les-Flots, Carnon and La Grande-Motte may provoke perplexity and even debate, it is easy to understand why some people prefer to turn their backs on these models of coastal mass tourism.

Others, fortunately, reserve some dazzling surprises. Although, when leaving Sète, you may choose to spend some time in Frontignan, the home of the famous Muscat, which, apart from its very beautiful fortified church (12th – 14th century) has an interesting local history museum, above all, you must not miss a long break at P.K. 79. A few hundred metres from the canal, built on a sort of peninsula attached to the coastline, stands the fortified church of Maguelone, the only remains of what, in the Middle Ages, was a powerful Episcopal city and port, the bridgehead of the Christian world against the Saracens and the refuge for several Popes during the war between the Priesthood and the Empire. But competition from Montpellier, which stole its bishopric in the 16th century, and the ravages of the Wars of Religion, were soon going to mark its decline. The dismantling of its fortifications, commissioned by Richelieu in 1622, and the dispersion of its ruins for the construction of the canal – the stones were either sold or thrown into the lagoons – finally turned it into

Bishops' tombs in Maguelone Cathedral.

A Dutch-style narrowboat in the port of Aigues-Mortes.

a ghost town. Of its former glory, now buried in the sand, today there remains only the solitary and nostalgic silhouette of the ancient cathedral, a sentinel from the past standing between sky and sea. On the other side of the canal, the visit to the very beautiful village of Villeneuve-lès-Maguelone, with its winding streets lined with medieval houses, is an indispensable addition to the visit to Maguelone.

But, it is 20 kilometres further on towards Beaucaire that the highlight of the route lies, when, in the distance, the towers and walls of Aigues-Mortes appear, a poignant, mineral solitude in a desert of marshes and lagoons, which Chateaubriand described as a "tall ship stranded in the sand". Born out of nothing in a setting from the end of the world where only poor fishermen used to go, it was built in 1240 by Saint Louis who wanted a fortified port to affirm his presence in the Mediterranean and, above all, a departure point for his crusades in the Holy Land. Aigues-Mortes

The Tour de Constance in Aigues-Mortes, commissioned by Saint Louis to reinforce the town's defences.

The Petite Camargue, a world of water without equal.

Near Aigues-Mortes, the Tour Carbonière stands isolated in the middle of flooded fields.

is unable to deny its war-mongering origins: its geometric layout – five longitudinal streets and five transversal streets dividing a 550-metre by 300-metre rectangle into regular blocks – its crenellated ramparts, its towers – the oldest one is the Tour de Constance which offers a magnificent viewpoint – and its fortified gates, mean that it is a remarkably well-preserved example of medieval military architecture. In spite of marsh fever, which regularly decimated its population, in spite of the recurring plague and cholera epidemics, in spite of the ravages of the Hundred Years War, Aigues-Mortes prospered for many long years. But, the decline which started in the 15th century with the irreversible silting of the channel between its port and the sea, the Wars of Religion, and, finally, the creation of the port of Sète, led to an agonisingly slow death. Nevertheless, its untouched beauty has crossed the centuries and tourism has now offered it a new lease of life.

After the splendours of Aigues-Mortes, you may fear that the canal has nothing more to offer. Not so. The crossing of the Petite Camargue, with its farmhouses lost in the elusive immensity of marshy plains, is a per-

Detail on the gate of Saint-Gilles Abbey, a masterpiece of Romanesque sculpture.

petual enchantment. Before Beaucaire, at least two stops must be made: the first stop is in Saint-Gilles, the ancient resting place on the Route of Santiago de Compostelle, with its streets lined with Romanesque houses and the abbey which, despite major damage during the Wars of Religion, has retained a façade considered to be a pure masterpiece of meridional Romanesque sculpture; the second stop is in Bellegarde, a

Saint-Gilles Abbey was built entirely in the 12th century, which provides it with outstanding architectural unity.

Bellegarde, a very ancient village dominated by the beautiful ruins of the Tour de la Madone.

Below:
Beaucaire.
The canal and quays.

very old hilltop village dominated by the Tour de la Madone, which offers a stunning viewpoint.

And then you are in Beaucaire, the final stage in the canal before its junction with the River Rhône. Beaucaire, straight out of a time when towns

The port of Beaucaire, Quai de la Paix: today a sleepy town, but in the past, for centuries, the site of one of the most famous fairs in France.

were made for people, with its shady and sun-filled streets, its hidden houses, its cheerful and flower-covered quaysides, its castle with the magnificent ruins dominating an ocean of pink and ochre-coloured roof tiles, and, on the other side of the River Rhone, the steeples and towers of its rival twin, Tarascon. Although it is no longer the rich city with its annual fair – the largest in France in the 18th century – which, every year, used to attract more than 300,000 visitors, each of its stones appears to have retained the memory of its former prosperity.

Below:
The Château of Tarascon, the twin city of Beaucaire on the left bank of the River Rhône.

Sea salt

General view.
© Salins du Midi.

The very first salt marshes may have been installed in the Rhone delta by the Phoenicians from the end of 2AD, and the Provence salt marsh works were already exporting their production in Roman times. But, it was only in the middle of the 13th century, at the time of its construction by Saint Louis, that salt marshes were developed near Aigues-Mortes. In this region, salt is obtained from seawater which is pumped into basins, unlike the salt marshes in the Atlantic where it is the power of the tides which fills the basins. Today, it is only the salt marshes in Lapalme, Sainte-Lucie, Gruissan and Aigues-Mortes which are active, with an annual capacity of about 1 million tons. With a surface area of 10,000 hectares, the Aigues-Mortes salt marshes alone provide 50% of this total.

- Visit to Aigues-Mortes Salt Marshes:
Visit aboard the "Petit Train des Sauniers" (from April to the end of October); Tel for information: 04 66 73 40 24
- Visit to Gruissan Salt Marshes (Aude): Tel. for information: 04 68 49 29 77

© Salins du Midi.

The Canal Latéral à la Garonne

We know that on Riquet's death, "the construction of the canal for navigation and communication between the Ocean and Mediterranean Seas" was not really completed. Travellers were still obliged to follow the River Garonne between Toulouse and Bordeaux, the capricious course of which led to frequent interruptions in traffic and, because it required the use of lighter vessels with less drag than those for navigating on the canal, involved a costly load transfer. In 1685, Vauban himself evoked the project of a minor canal to the Garonne, the only solution to this joint problem. But, it was necessary to wait until the middle of the 19th century for this project to finally become a reality, although not without some difficulties. Started in 1839, the works were interrupted several times, in particular because of pressure from the rail lobby which wanted to transform an already completed section of the water route into a railway line. "The government was wise enough not to cede to uninformed suggestions coming from all directions: it refused to destroy a construction which so successfully completed Riquet's work [1]."

Opened in successive sections – Toulouse-Montech, Montech-Moissac, Moissac-Aiguillon, Aiguillon-Castets-en-Dorthe – the canal was completed in 1856. Between Toulouse and Castets-en-Dorthe, where it joins the River Garonne – now easily navigable for the approximately 53 kilometres remaining to reach Bordeaux – it covers 193.5 kilometres, is crossed by 159 bridges and has 53 locks – updated in the 1970s to the "Freycinet gauge" in order to accommodate 38.50 metre-long barges – for a total altitude difference of slightly more than 110 metres. From Montech, an 11-kilometre branch canal (9 bridges, 10 locks, 20-metre altitude difference) provides access to Montauban. Currently out of service, it will very soon be reopened to navigation.

The fame of its prestigious elder, the Canal du Midi, the strong identity of the regions and towns passed through by the Canal de la Robine and the Canal du Rhône à Sète mean that sometimes it is forgotten that the Canal Latéral à la Garonne – which, we admit is not done any great service by its official name – is one of the most beautiful navigable ways in France and could be the subject of an "Itinéraire de Découvertes" on its own.

The Canal Latéral à la Garonne at Hure.

Below:
Peyrets Lock in Montech.

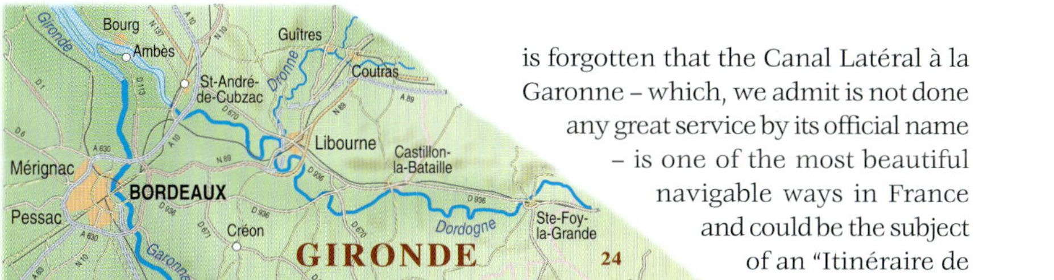
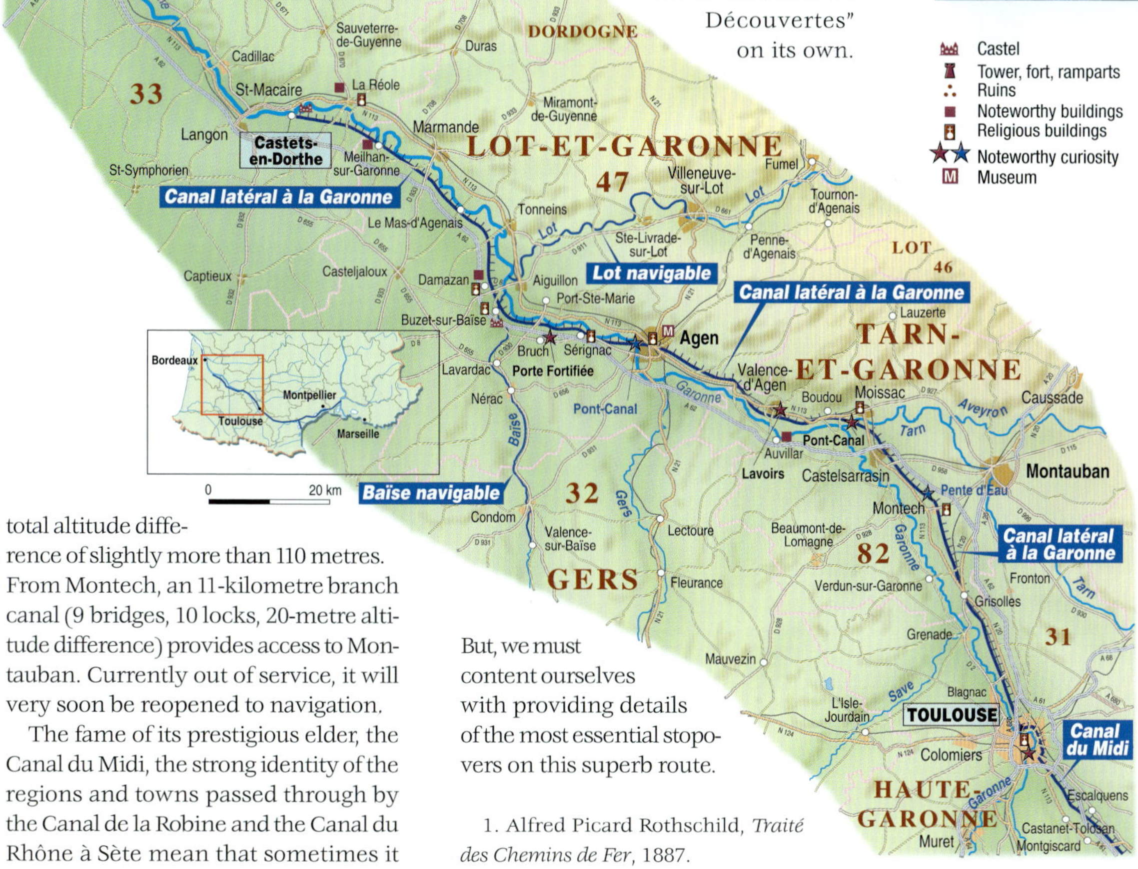

But, we must content ourselves with providing details of the most essential stopovers on this superb route.

1. Alfred Picard Rothschild, *Traité des Chemins de Fer*, 1887.

The water slope in Montech and its two electric railcars.

Montech

Although the old town is worth a visit for its old houses and its Church of Notre-Dame-de-la-Visitation, above all it is the "water slope" which is of interest to us. This device, which was a worldwide first when put into service in 1974 and which is unique in Europe, enables barges to pass an altitude difference of 13.30 metres without passing through five consecutive locks. The principle is as follows: a 125-metre "corner of water" held downstream by a mobile "mask" towed by two electric railcars, ascends or descends the 3% slope along a 443-metre channel. Thus, instead of boats passing from reach to reach, it is the reach itself which moves. Not only does this system allow barges and passenger boats – pleasure boats are not allowed to use it – to change altitude in 20 minutes instead of 65 minutes through the five locks, it also does not involve the use of any water since it is not necessary to empty the reach as in an ordinary lock.

Moissac

It is after having crossed the Tarn along the superb 356-metre long brick and stone canal bridge in Cacor, that we reach this small town, which would be relatively ordinary if it were not home to two treasures. The first is the famous golden Chasselas, a sweet and aromatic grape from the vines growing on its slopes. The second is its abbey, the cloister of which is considered to be one of the most beautiful – if not the most beautiful – in the world. The very fact that it is still visible today is a miracle in itself in view of the incredible

Moissac Lock.

The port of Castelsarrasin.

The cloister of Moissac Abbey is said to be the most beautiful in the world.

Detail from the southern door of Saint-Pierre abbatial.

series of misfortunes which has struck it: founded in the 6th or 7th century, it was pillaged successively by the Saracens, then the Normans, sacked by Simon de Montfort, ravaged during the Hundred Years War and the Wars of Religion and vandalised in the reign of Terror. And, as if all that were not enough, it was almost demolished last century to make way for the railway line. Nevertheless, Moissac Abbey continues to be dazzling. The 11th century cloister, with its four vaulted galleries resting on sixty-six arches and its columns with sculpted capitals, as well as the southern door of the old Saint-Pierre abbatial, with its tympanum illustrating the Apocalypse of Saint Jean, are one of the purest masterpieces of Romanesque art.

Cacor canal bridge enables the Canal Latéral à la Garonne to reach Moissac over the Tarn.

The rich countryside in the region of Moissac.

Boudou

A short detour through this small village (drop anchor between P.K. 70 and 71) will not disappoint: the view over the confluence of the Tarn and the Garonne is of the utmost beauty.

Auvillar

Even if it means having to travel almost 5 kilometres from Pommevic Lock (P.K. 78) do not hesitate to do so. Auvillar, built in pink brick, with its beautiful 17th and 18th century houses, its curious round covered market and its viewpoint over the Garonne, is rightfully said to be one of the jewels of Tarn-et-Garonne.

Valence-d'Agen

This ancient bastide – it was founded in the 13th century – has much charm. From its past there still

The confluence of the Tarn and the Garonne seen from Boudou viewpoint.

remains, apart from the geometric layout of its streets, three beautiful wash-houses which on their own make the visit worthwhile.

Agen

The largest town on the route obviously demands a long stopover. A little modern perhaps? It is true that those who enjoy old stones may not find the same pleasures here as in Toulouse, Carcassonne or Béziers, even if, in addition to Saint-Caprais Cathedral (12th century) there are some very beautiful old timber-framed houses and elegant townhouses. But, the town is so harmonious with its quaysides, its shaded squares and its wide avenues and life is so pleasant – was it not chosen as first in France for quality of life? – that it is a pleasure to spend some time there.

Bastide of Valence-d'Agen, one of the old public wash-houses (13th century), one of the most interesting monuments inf the town.

Agen. A narrowboat crosses the canal bridge.

The monumental canal bridge over the Garonne in Agen.

Agen. Canal on the Garonne and on the Midi Bordeaux-Sète line.

Agen.
Canal bridge lock.

Do not miss a visit to the Museum of Fine Arts, situated in an admirable series of four adjoining 16th and 17th century townhouses, home to an outstanding archaeology, gold work, porcelain and painting collection from the 18th, 19th and 20th centuries. At the western exit of Agen, navigators will be able to admire the longest canal bridge in France – and without a doubt one of the most beautiful – with its twenty-three 20-metre wide arches which cross the Garonne over a majestic span of 580 metres.

Sérignac

The church in this small bastide has a very unusual helicoid bell tower. Built in 1546, it was damaged by lightning and restored in 1922, and again in 1988. Legend has it that, having been destroyed by the devil three times, it was given this shape to fasten it securely into the sky.

Agen prunes

With their black and shiny wrinkled skin, creamy flesh ranging from golden yellow to amber, and delicately sweet taste, Agen prunes have, for many long years, been a culinary success. It is to monks – those from Clairac Abbey – that we owe this delicious treat. Plum trees carried to the Lot valley from Syria by crusaders were, initially, grafted on to indigenous plum trees probably as early as the 12th century. The Ente plums obtained were of such quality that their production spread very quickly. But their season was short. How was it possible to keep them so that they could be eaten all year round? Our clever monks had the idea of steaming them, drying them and then storing them in the dark in order to prevent the development of mould. The prune was born. It is not quite fair that Agen has given its name to this delicacy, because the fruit is harvested mainly in the region of Villeneuve-sur-Lot. However, they used to be bought by traders from Agen, before being shipped by waterway to Bordeaux, from where they travelled to England, a country which consumed large quantities of them. That is the reason for the confusion between the place of consignment and the place of production.
Ente plums are harvested from 25 August to 25 September once they have taken their fill of the summer sun.
Although, traditionally, they were harvested by hand after the tree was shaken, the process has become increasingly mechanised. After harvesting, they are dried and 3 kilos of fresh plums give a final total of 1 kilo of prunes. The title of "pruneaux d'Agen" is reserved exclusively for those made with the Ente plum, the orchards of which cover 16,500 hectares.

Agen.
Canal du Midi.

Bruch

This beautiful enclosed village, 1.5 kilometres from Auvignon Lock, can be spotted from a distance thanks to its impressive fortified medieval gateway.

Buzet-sur-Baïse

We already know the highly worthy wines of "Côtes de Buzet" which have forged the reputation of this small winemaking centre. But, just as much as its wineries, it is its site on the banks of the canal and the River Baïse, its 13th and 14th century church and its superb castle (private property), dominating the plain from the top of its rocky outcrop, which justifies a stopover.

Damazan

This ancient English bastide has retained some interesting remains from its past: timber-framed houses, a townhouse with a very beautiful 14th century staircase and part of its ramparts.

Agen Lock: here, we understand what the difficulties presented by the terrain were.

Next to Meilhan, the Canal Latéral and the Garonne are only separated by a few dozen metres.

Le Mas-d'Agenais

Founded in Roman times, the antique Velenum Pompejacum has offered up several archaeological treasures, including the Vénus du Mas, exhibited at Agen Museum of Fine Arts. Its exceptional site overlooking the Garonne and the canal, its Romanesque gateway, its 17th century covered wheat market and, above all, Saint-Vincent Church (12th century), reputed to be one of the most beautiful built south of the Garonne, which houses a Christ on the cross by Rembrandt, all make it an unmissable stopover.

Tersac

Downstream from Bernès Lock, on the left bank of the canal, stands a stunning 12th century chapel, indisputably one of the most photogenic on the route.

Meilhan-sur-Garonne

From the terraces of this ancient Gallo-Roman town, the view over the Garonne valley is of supreme beauty. The remains of its ramparts and its citadel – dismantled in 1622 on the orders of Richelieu – deserve a visit.

La Réole

On the right bank of the Garonne, 2 kilometres from the canal, La Réole was a major port where "*gabares*" (scows) used to load and unload wheat, fruit, vegetables and spirits. Of its monastic origins – it grew up around an abbey in the 9th century – it has retained the Gothic Saint-Pierre Church (13th century), the former abbatial Benedictine chapel, and the 18th century conventual buildings. But, La Réole was also an important military stronghold: evidence of this can be seen in the ruins of the ramparts and the imposing Château of Les Quat'Sos, the remains of a citadel built in the 13th century by Henry III of England. The town hall from the start of the 13th century – the oldest in France – and several attractive Medieval, Renaissance and Classic houses complete a very rich and well-restored collection of monuments.

Meilhan offers a superb viewpoint.

Castets-en-Dorthe

Terminus! It is in this beautiful village, dominated by the walls and watchtowers of a 14th century castle, that the canal joins the Garonne. We will not fail to salute it one last time from the terrace situated behind the church from which there is a magnificent view over the valley.

The port of Castets-en-Dorthe where the Canal Latéral meets the Garonne.

On the Garonne...

Château of Malromé, former property of Toulouse-Lautrec.

Over the 53 kilometres separating Castets-en-Dorthe from Bordeaux, the Garonne is now tamed and easy to navigate, although the presence of some sizeable vessels – barges and push tugs – demands unfailing attention. Noble landscapes, vineyards, towns of art and castles, the route has no reason to be envious of the one through which we have already passed.

Street in Saint-Macaire.

Although there are many tempting ports-of-call, here we have retained just a few of them. You will be dazzled by Saint-Macaire, which dominates the river from the top of its rocky promontory and which has retained its medieval appearance so well that the town appears to have been caught in a time warp on the riverbank. In an atmosphere reminiscent of "Thérèse Desqueyroux", you will fall under the charm of Malagar Manor, where François Mauriac used to live, 1 kilometre from the small village of Verdelais... From the viewpoint at Sainte-Croix-du-Mont, enjoy the vast panorama over the valley and the

Hauts de Langoiran vineyards.

vineyards. In Cadillac, marvel at the square lined with archways, the Gothic church and the castle built in the 17th century by the Duke of Épernon. And, finally, the fortifications of Rions, the ruins of the fortress in Langoiran and the fortified church of Boulac, the last stages before arriving in Bordeaux, the beautiful, secretive and aristocratic capital of Aquitaine.

The Pont de Pierre in Bordeaux symbolises all the pride of the capital of Aquitaine.

Porte de Lhyan (12th century) in Rions.

The Chartrons district in Bordeaux.

Two navigable rivers: the Lot and the Baïse

The feat represented by the Atlantic-Mediterranean junction of the Two Seas Canal, and the extraordinary economic boom which it generated, must not allow us to forget the historic importance of river navigation in the Southwest long before its construction. Since Antiquity, fleets of vessels of all sorts, from rafts to scows, have followed the dense network of waterways, including those which, today, appear to be too rapid or too narrow to be navigable. On the banks of the Adour, the Garonne, the

Castel
Tower, fort, ramparts
Ruins
Noteworthy buildings
Religious buildings
Noteworthy curiosity
Museum

Left page: **The Lot valley seen from the eagle's nest of Penne-d'Agenais.**

The banks of the River Baïse in Condom.

Dordogne, the Aveyron, the Tarn, the Lot and the Baïse, dozens of ports prospered where winemakers, farmers and traders entrusted their goods to sailors who carried them to the major trading centres, running the risk of rapids and shallows. The railway and, later, the road led to the demise off these "river professions" – carpenters, towers, porters, sailors, inn-keepers – which employed thousands of men and women, and, last century, many rivers - at least those which were most difficult to navigate – ceased to be "corridors of life".

Tourism saved the Canal du Midi and yet again it is tourism which has helped to bring life back to this important piece of our history and heritage which is river navigation. Thanks to tourism, abandoned rivers have been restored to life, sleepy villages have awoken and condemned locks have been put back into service.

Thus, in the past few years, the Lot and the Baïse, which have been progressively cleared, have been returned to their liveliness of former times. All the more accessible because they are joined to the Canal Latéral à la Garonne, they offer the opportunity to follow the "route of silence" and access some of the most beautiful landscapes in France.

The Lot

Already two sections of the Lot have been restored to navigation. The first, from Saint-Cirq-Lapopie to Luzech, covers 64.3 kilometres and comprises fourteen locks. The second, from Villeneuve-sur-Lot to Nicole, from where, along the Garonne, it is possible to reach the mouth of the Baïse, covers 51.8 kilometres and comprises three locks.

From Saint-Cirq-Lapopie to Cahors

Sublime. It is the only word which comes to mind when discovering this magical place. "More than any other site – in America or Europe – Saint-Cirq has cast a spell over me: one which has settled me forever. I have ceased to want to be elsewhere. I believe that the secret of its poetry is similar to certain illuminations by Rimbaud", wrote André Breton. Hanging vertiginously on the promontory which sits 100 metres above the Lot, houses, towers and steeples with brown and ochre-coloured tiles appear to remain in place by a miracle of balance. In the steeply sloping streets, everything is to be marvelled at: the gardens hanging on tiny terraces, the Gothic windows, the corbelled facades, the magnificent views over the valley crushed between the cliffs. We could talk about the history of Saint-Cirq-Lapopie, evoke the three castles of its three suzerain families, recall the legendary skill of the artisans which made it wealthy in the Middle Ages. But is that really what is important when compared to the pure emotion generated by the incomparable beauty of this village straight out of a storybook?

Hanging vertiginously above the River Lot, the village of Saint-Cirq-Lapopie is among the most beautiful in France.

Quercy Lamb

On the stark limestone plateaux of Quercy, the grass is perfumed and sweet, but is sparse. Only hardy breeds, able to cover untiringly the vast and meagre pastures are able to survive. This is the case of the "caussenard" sheep, with its long legs, "glasses" and black ears, making it easily recognisable. The ewe produces two lambs per litter. Fed with mother's milk, then with a complement of cereal and hay, they weigh about 18 kilos by the age of 100 days. According to connoisseurs, the quality of the meat and the flavour of Quercy farm lamb is to be found nowhere else.

The cliffs along the Lot valley between Saint-Cirq-Lapopie and Bouziès.

Downstream from Saint-Cirq, the river cuts a difficult path between the high cliffs. Hilltop villages, mills, strange troglodyte castles which, according to legend, were the work of the Devil, or the English – a plausible reminder of the Hundred Years War – at every bend, the changing landscapes are perpetually enchanting.

There are too many sites deserving of a stopover or a short excursion to be able to describe them all. Let us highlight the most spectacular. About 2 kilometres from Saint-Cirq, on the left bank, is the start of a 700-metre towpath cut into the cliff face, the creation of which by an unknown group of people, is surely one of the most stupefying in the history of river navigation; opposite, the sentinel castles of Conduché and Condat appear to continue their watch over the confluence of the Lot and the Célé. On the right bank, at Bouziès bridge, in the steep "défilé des Anglais", appears a troglodyte castle, excavated in the Middle Ages out of caves in the cliff, with doors which could only be

Cahors seen from Mont Saint-Cyr.

reached by ladder. Slightly further on appears the silhouette of the hilltop village of Bouziès-Bas, dominated by the dovecote of its 16th century manor. After a series of hairpin bends, it is the turn of Vers, set on a superb site at the confluence of the Lot and the small river which gave its name to the village, to offer the remains of two castles, one an "Englishman's castle", and a Roman aqueduct. In the same way as sailors in former times, for whom it was a pilgrimage site, we will not forget to stop a few hundred metres downstream, in front of Notre-Dame-de-Velles Romanesque chapel. Between Vers and Lacombe Lock, although the Tour de Galessie, which, perched on the top of its rock, overhangs the Lot, and the village of Laroque-des-Arcs, with its Saint-Roch chapel, its 13th century keep and its "Englishman's castle" are unforgettable sites, above all it is the "bories" built on each bank which are of interest to us. Elsewhere, "bories" are simple, isolated, dry-stone huts found in fields and used for storage or shelter. Here, they are magnificent homes, built from the 13th century by the "Caorsins", traders who made huge fortunes from silver and fabrics. Although the oldest of them are reminiscent of strongholds, with ramparts and a keep, the more recent ones, dating from the 14th century, are true palaces. The most spectacular ones can be seen in Savanac and Reganhac.

Cahors

Enclosed as if on a peninsula in a loop in the River Lot, Cahors is more than simply beautiful. It has been touched by grace. It is not very often that a town provokes such amazement through the incredible moving harmony of its architecture, the charm of its streets and squares and the elegance and power of its monuments. It could have become a museum town, made sterile by over meticulous restoration, polluted by the parasites of historic trash and temple merchants selling pieces of the past, but, that is not the case. And,

The old town of Cahors.

Old Cahors seen from the loop in the Lot.

Valentré fortified bridge (14th century) has become the emblem of Cahors.

that is why it is not possible to devote less than one day of exquisite wandering to it. Set off without a programme and allow yourself to be absorbed. No doubt, you will discover it on your own and without tiring yourself – Cahors comes from a time when towns were made for pedestrians – as you move from street to street between the districts of Badernes and Soubirous, Valentré bridge, Saint-Étienne Cathedral, Saint-Barthélemy Church, the King's Castle and Duèze Palace.

Valentré tower bridge.

From Cahors to Luzech

The Lot appears to have shaken off the cliffs which have surrounded it until now and wends its way through a wide valley where vineyards and fields of tobacco flourish, through a multitude of "cingles", namely meanders, between strongholds, villages, each more beautiful than the last, castles – there are no fewer than ten within 18 kilometres – mills and churches. In Pardines, the ruins of the fortress, the "borie" of Englandières and, above all, Saint-Martial Church, which, in the Middle Ages, was a major pilgrimage centre, largely justify a stopover. Further downstream, Mercuès can be seen from far off, thanks to its castle dominating the valley from the top of its promontory. Built in the 13th century and later extended in several successive phases, in particular in the 14th and 16th centuries, this former residence of the Prince-Bishops of Cahors has now been turned into a hotel. Until Douelle, each "cingle" reveals a new treasure: these are successively the Château of Bouysses (right bank), Marthre "borie" (left bank), the Château of Cessac (right bank), Flaynac Chapel (left bank) and, finally, the Château of Carriol (right

Cahors Wine

It used to be called "black wine" and from the Middle Ages to the 13th century it was hugely famous. Clément Marot sang about the virtues of this "fiery liquor", François I liked it so much that he entrusted the winemakers of Cahors with creating the vineyard at Fontainebleau, the Russian Orthodox Church chose it for mass wine, and Colbert did not hesitate to declare it to be better than Bordeaux. Sic transit gloria mundi. Gradually, Cahors wine was forgotten, before, at the end of the 19th century, phylloxera led to its complete disappearance. The recovery has been slow and difficult and only recently the reputation of these wines was still worse than bad. Too many winemakers contented themselves with making "the vines piss" and producing an abundance of easy wines without any character. But, everything has changed in the past twenty years. "At the start of the 1980s, a new generation of winemakers took matters in hand, defining an elegant and vigorous style for the modern-day Cahors", wrote the major wine critics Desseauve and Bettane.

For two thousand years, the basic vine stock has been "cot noir" – locally known as Auxerrois – which gives Cahors its tannin taste and its dark red colour. The rest either comprises Merlot, which gives it body, or Tannat, which accentuates its qualities as a cellar wine. When young, it has a wild and coarse taste, and, after two years, becomes fuller and more vigorous. An excellent cellar wine, the best vintages may be kept until 15 years of age and over. It is a perfect accompaniment to roasted meat, game, cheese and red fruit, as well as the main dishes of the Lot, such as farm-style lamb and truffle omelette.

The vineyards: Cahors is experiencing a full recovery.

Keep of the Episcopal Château of Luzech (12th century).

bank). We will not fail to drop anchor for a while at Douelle, with its imposing quaysides and the small votive boat in its church reminding us that this village, which appears so modest today, was, in the last century, the most active port on the Lot between Cahors and Fumel. Before Luzech, at last, you will rest your eyes on the medieval Château of Laroque, the Romanesque church of Caillac – with its particularly remarkable Renaissance door – the Château of Langle (15th – 16th century) and the Château of Caïx (17th century), currently the property of the Danish royal family.

Luzech, set in an almost perfect loop in the Lot — at its narrowest part, the strip of land is barely one hundred metres wide – offers an unforgettable display: nestling at the foot of the "pech de l'Impernal", a steep hill which holds the remains of a Gallo-Roman oppidum, it still retains elements from its glorious past, such as a stronghold, a 12th century keep, remarkably well-preserved medieval districts, and a flamboyant Gothic-style church, Notre-Dame-de-l'Isle, which, the same as the one in Douelle, holds an ex-voto for sailors.

For the moment, Luzech marks the end of the journey. Until Villeneuve-sur-Lot, navigation is practically impossible. But, rehabilitation projects – which require long and costly works – will succeed. No doubt, in a few years time, small narrowboats and other live-aboard vessels will be able to travel along the Lot without stopping between Saint-Cirq-Lapopie and the Garonne.

From Villeneuve-sur-Lot to the Garonne

In its lower course, the Lot becomes lazier and its meanders widen in a valley which has become increasingly large. No doubt less picturesque than the section from Saint-Cirq-Lapopie to Luzerch, this route does, nevertheless, offer many admirable landscapes and magnificent stopovers.

Villeneuve-sur-Lot

Bastide founded in 1253 and built in the space of just fifteen years, this attractive small town has retained, apart from its two fortified gates, the remains of its old ramparts, a magnificent 13th century "Pont Vieux" and a large collection of medieval buildings.

Villeneuve-sur-Lot: a very ancient bastide.

The suspended houses of Villeneuve-sur-Lot at Pont Vieux.

The stark architecture of the commandery of the Templar Knights at Temple-sur-Lot.

Casseneuil

A former river port on a peninsula at the confluence of the Lède and the Lot, with terraced gardens and delightful timber-framed houses suspended over the river.

Sainte-Livrade

The Tour Richard-Cœur-de-Lion, which succeeded in saving its ramparts, and the Romanesque chevet in the parish church make a stopover worthwhile.

Le Temple-sur-Lot

Formerly the seat of a commandery of the Templar Knights, this small, peaceful town has retained a beautiful building dating from the 15th century.

Castelmoron

The small town centre has several interesting old houses. The banks of the Lot and the marina bustle with life. About 4 kilometres away, the delightful hilltop village of Laparade offers a magnificent view over the valley.

The banks of the Lot at Castelmoron.

Granges-sur-Lot

Its original Prune Museum – emblematic product of the region – is well worth a visit.

Clairac

A superb stopover, one of the most beautiful on the route. Although many of the old houses are still awaiting a face-lift, the Benedictine abbey, the reason for the village's foundation, has been restored superbly. The village's Automaton Museum is a visit not to be missed.

Aiguillon

A former Roman castrum which watches over the confluence of the Lot and the Garonne from the top of

Timber-framed house in Clairac.

A narrow street in Clairac: a medieval building in need of some attentive restoration.

Aiguillon Mill on the Baïse.

its promontory, and, later, a stronghold disputed by the English and French during the Hundred Years War, the town experienced its period of greatest prosperity in the 18th century when the Duke of Aiguillon, in disgrace at Court, turned it into a small capital of society and culture. Next to the impressive mass of the classic-style castle, started in 1765 but never completed, are the remains of a delightful small neighbourhood with narrow streets lined with timber-framed houses.

Nicole

It is at the foot of this ancient English bastide that the Lot joins the Garonne. Less than 1 kilometre away, the viewpoint in Bachot offers a magnificent panorama. From Nicole Lock, which may be reached along a narrow canal from Aiguillon Lock, it is possible to join the mouth of the Baïse, provided that you use the services of a tug (regular toll service) to cross and sail up the Garonne.

Porte de Vianne, a fortified bastide which is one of the most beautiful in the region.

The haughty and severe grace of the Château of Xaintrailles.

Upriver along the Baïse

It is so modest and discreet that you may be astonished, but the Baïse was a trade route of prime importance in the Middle Ages. Here, every year, for centuries, small vessels, adapted to the narrowness and shallow draught of the river, transported thousands of tons of goods, wheat, cork, flour, tobacco, wine and Armagnac, along the river. The passage from reach to reach was along simple pathways, before basic wooden locks, time-consuming and difficult to handle, were installed in the 17th century. It was necessary to wait until the Second Empire – when the traffic reached 130,000 tons – for these to be replaced with "modern" locks, still in use today.

Lavardac Mill.

Sailing upriver along the Baïse from Buzet-sur-Baïse, is a wonderful journey through the region of the Cadets de Gascogne, manor houses, bastides, foie gras and Armagnac, in landscapes so civilised and cheerful that it is impossible to doubt that it is well and truly here and nowhere else that "happiness is in the fields".

Today, the Baïse is navigable from Saint-Léger to Valence-sur-Baïse, namely a 58-kilometre journey comprising 20 locks.

After Saint-Léger double lock, the gateway from the river for boats coming from the Garonne, an initial reach (4.600 kilometres) leads to Buzet-sur-Baïse (see chapter 5). The next reach (10.500 kilometres) initially runs parallel to the Canal Latéral before crossing it and passing below a canal bridge and heading southwards. At the end of this second reach, you will not regret taking a break at Vianne: this delightful bastide mirrored in the Baïse presents, apart from remarkable architectural unity, the unique feature of having retained its fortifications

Fortified mill in Barbaste.

The old town of Nérac.

intact. After this, stop at Lavardac, a former port where, at one time, goods were transferred between boats with shallow draught, the only ones able to navigate upstream and those with greater tonnage, which headed downstream to join the Garonne. Near this small town, Barbaste is worth an excursion: its mill, fortified in the 12th and 13th centuries, flanked with four square towers and a Romanesque bridge with ten arches is of rare beauty.

Four locks and a few meanders remain before one of the gems on the route. Nérac has forgotten nothing of

Henri IV castle, where, in the Albret period, a brilliant court lived.

its period of splendour when, as capital of Albret, it played host to poets, humanists and scholars around Margaret of Navarre, or when Antoine de Bourbon and Jeanne d'Albret lived here, the creators of the future Vert-Galant. On each side of the Baïse, linked by the humpback of Pont Vieux, the two parts of the old town – Petit Nérac and the castle's neighbourhood – have retained an extraordinarily authentic charm, even if Henri IV's castle has lost three of its four wings.

Timber-framed houses in the old town of Nérac.

Lock on the Baïse in Nérac.

Statue of Fleurette, one of Henri IV's loves.

Street sign in Moncrabeau.

The "liar's chair" in Moncrabeau.

Upstream from Nérac, the course of the Baïse, between slopes and hills, becomes so tortuous and indecisive that many of its meanders have been altered with canals. Exquisite wandering: on each bank, through bright and peaceful landscapes, Gascony farmhouses with large tiled roofs, manors and castles with parks shaded with huge cedars glide past. Before arriving in Condom, take a short break in Moncrabeau, which made its name by proclaiming itself to be the "world capital of liars". Organised by the Academy of Liars, founded in the 18th century, a lying contest is held here every year, with a funny face championship every three years. From Rue Cocu-Saute to Place de la Mentherie Royale, a "liar's circuit" even offers an opportunity to discover the village.

A more flattering title than that of *Sous-Préfecture* of Gers, above all, Condom is the capital of Armagnac. Therefore, a long stopover is essential. Take time to stroll through the network of medieval streets in its ancient neighbourhoods – fortunately now largely pedestrianised – admire the Gothic Saint-Pierre Cathedral, the Bishops' Chapel and the many beautiful townhouses – for example those of Polignac, Bourran

Condom, capital of Armagnac, and not, as its name may suggest, of condoms.

The banks of the Baïse in Condom.

and Cugnac – and visit the Armagnac Museum. Although the etymology of the town's name – Condatomagus, the "market of Condus" (Gallo-Roman men's name) – has nothing whatsoever to do with the English word condom, the village has made amusing use of this confusion by organising an exhibition every summer on the theme of this method of contraception.

How to read a label

The ageing reference always concerns the youngest spirit in the blend.
"Trois Étoiles": Armagnac with at least two years of ageing in wood. "V.O.", "V.S.O.P." or "Réserve": Armagnac with at least five years of ageing in wood. "Extra", "Napoléon", "Vieille Réserve" or "X.O.": Armagnac with at least six years of ageing in wood.
"Hors d'Age": Armagnac with at least ten years of ageing in wood.
The vintage corresponds exclusively to the year of harvest referred to on the label.

Armagnac

With its gently rounded hills, its sleepy villages and its gentle horizons, the land of Armagnac gives you your money's worth. How is it possible to believe that such a peaceful and civilised country has signed a pact with water, fire, God, the angels and the Devil? Every year, insomniac alchemists lead a sabbath of witches between retorts and stills. And, every year their cauldrons bring forth a celestial spirit, the most perfect ever designed by men. Invasions do have a good side and Armagnac is proof of this: if the Gauls, the inventors of the barrel, had not been defeated by the Romans, there would have been no vineyards in Gascony; if the Arabs had not continued an incursion as far as Poitiers, there would have been no stills. Without vines, barrels, or stills, there would have been no Armagnac. QED. Even the English became involved: by forbidding Dutch ships from sailing up the Garonne to load wines from the upper regions of Gascony, they forced winemakers to distil part of their harvest in order to ensure its conservation. Some of the strange quirks of history which have given rise to this divine drink. Armagnac is obtained by distilling white wines from eleven grape varieties, mainly Ugni Blanc, Colombard, Folle Blanche and Baco Blanc. It is distilled continuously in Armagnacais pure hammered copper stills, consecrated in 1818 by a patent granted by Louis XVIII. As soon as it is removed from the still, Armagnac is placed in 400 to 420-litre oak casks - "pièces" – in which the new wood gradually gives it aromas and tannin. It is then transferred to older casks to complete the ageing process, during which time its alcohol content diminishes through continuous evaporation, called the "angels' share". Once the storehouse manager considers the ageing to be sufficient, he carries out "cuts", namely the blending of several spirits of different origins and ages. Armagnac is sold with a minimum alcohol content of 40% volume and, therefore, is diluted with successive phases of "petites eaux" prepared in secret in the storehouses. Nevertheless, some old Armagnacs, most often vintages, are sold with their natural alcohol content at the end of ageing.

The Ryst-Dupeyron Armagnac storehouse in Condom.

Braziac Lock.

It is in Valence-sur-Baïse, about ten kilometres south of Condom, that the Baïse is no longer navigable. However, the journey ends in beauty: at the foot of this bastide founded in the 13th century, which has retained among the remains of its ramparts, a very beautiful fortified gate and a 15th century church with unusual octagonal towers, stands Flaran Abbey, a masterpiece of Cistercian art, at least comparable in its perfection to Fontfroide or Sénanque. Founded in the middle of the 12th century by Cistercians, it is a miraculous survivor of history: after escaping destruction in the Hundred Years War and the Wars of Religion, being sold as national property in the Revolution, it was still used as a warehouse thirty years ago. Magnificently restored, today it is considered to be one of the most beautiful religious edifices in the south of France.

The cloister of the Cistercian abbey of Flaran, a miraculous survivor of history, fortunately restored to perfection.

This trip up the Baïse brings to an end a long journey along the canals and rivers of Aquitaine, Midi-Pyrénées and Languedoc-Roussillon. On this journey along the Canal du Midi, the Canal de la Robine, the Canal du Rhône à Sète, the Canal Latéral à la Garonne, the Lot and the Baïse, we have covered more than 740 kilometres and passed through 170 locks. And, no doubt, acquired the conviction that the "routes of silence" help to offer a new look at some of the most beautiful regions of France.

Foie gras

It is a source of contention for animal lovers – especially Anglo-Saxons – who would like to prohibit it on the pretext that force-feeding is a barbarity inflicted on defenceless geese and ducks. True. But, whether uncooked, cooked or half-cooked, accompanied with truffles or not, fried with a few grapes or two halves of fig, spread on a fresh French stick, or a slice of toasted country-style bread, foie gras is such a masterpiece that we forget that, after all, foie gras is nothing more than a liver made sick through the gourmet ingenuity of men. You may be surprised, but it is true: foie gras is not protected by a label or the equivalent of an A.O.C., and nothing prevents it from being made in Brittany, Les Ardennes, Hungary or Israel. But, let it be said: apart from the magnificent Alsatian exception, whether it is goose or duck, the only truly great foie gras comes from the Southwest of France.

Cistercian abbey of Flaran.
Wall paintings (12th century).

Bibliography

Le Canal du Midi, histoire d'un chef d'œuvre, René Gast and Bruno Barbier, Ed. Ouest-France, 2006.

Le Canal des Deux Mers, André Maistre, Ed. Privat, 1968.

Connaissance du Canal du Midi, Arnaud d'Antin de Vaillac, Ed. France-Empire, 1997.

Le Canal du Midi, Francis Loubatières, Ed. Loubatières, 1997.

Le Canal du Midi, Jean-Denis Bergasse et Michel Adgé, Ed. Tallandier, 1989.

Le Canal du Midi et le canal latéral à la Garonne, Louis Destrem, Ed. du Chêne, 1996.

Canaux de France, Michel-Paul Simon, Ed. du Chêne, 1997.

Guides du Routard : Midi-Pyrénées, Languedoc-Roussillon, Ed. Hachette.

Guides Verts Michelin : *Pyrénées-Aquitaine-Côte basque, Pyrénées-Roussillon-Albigeois, Gorges du Tarn-Cévennes-Bas-Languedoc, Périgord-Quercy, Provence.*

Acknowledgements

To Françoise Cabanne and Patricia de Pouzilhac.

To the archivists at the Paul-Dupuy Museum and *Voies Navigables de France* in Toulouse.

To Crown Blue Line, which allowed us to navigate in comfort along the Canals of the Midi.

To Jacques Noisette from *Voies Navigables de France* in Toulouse.

The canal at Capestang.

PORKY PIG

CANALS AND NAVIGABLE WATERWAYS IN FRANCE

Practical guide for the amateur sailor

Navigation on canals and rivers

(© VNF Pierre Cheuva)

The Canal du Centre.

There are several options available for those wishing to navigate France's waterway network. The most popular is the tour boat, which allows you to explore a limited section of a canal or river for just a few hours. The archetypal tour boat is the Parisian *bateau-mouche*, whose tremendous success has made the French capital the world's leading tourist port. And on the Loire, the Dordogne, the Charente and the Canal du Midi, sailboats both traditional and modern offer excursions with a flavour of yesteryear. Hotel barges, which hold around twenty passengers, often offer luxurious services, with comfortable cabins, top-quality cuisine and guided tours of tourist attractions, for cruises lasting from a couple of days to a week. These boats mostly travel on the Canal du Midi and the Canal de Bourgogne.
River steamers are huge vessels – up to a hundred metres long, with a hundred cabins, one or more promenade decks, lounges and on-board entertainment – based on ocean cruise ships. Their size means that they can only navigate the wide-gauge network, in particular the Seine, the Rhine, the Rhône and the Saône.
Finally, house-boats under fifteen metres long can accommodate between two and twelve passengers. They can be hired for a weekend, a half-week or a week. A licence is not required for these boats: after an introductory session lasting less than an hour, the boat hire company issues a "provisional sailing certificate" which acts as a licence. There are currently over two thousand boats of this type on the French waterway network, from the most basic to the most luxurious. Their gauge means that they can be driven both on rivers and even the oldest canals, such as the Canal de Briare and the Canal du Midi.

(© VNF Pascal Lemaître)

The Rhine

The house-boat, a real home from home

There are 170 types of house-boat on the French waterway network – you will be spoilt for choice. The catalogues issued by boat hire companies are generally very detailed, with very clear plans giving you all the information you need to choose your boat. Rather than making your choice on the basis of the boat's appearance, it is advisable to choose your boat according to a number of criteria:

— price*, which varies depending on capacity, type of boat, season and region. Hiring a basic 6 to 8 metre (2 to 4 people) boat for one week will cost around €700 in very low season and around €1,000 in very high season, whereas hiring a "comfort" category 13 to 15 metre (8 to 10 people) boat will cost around €,500 in very low season and around €4,000 in very high season;

— the number of passengers. Note: a boat intended for 10 or 12 people does not have 10 or 12 cabins! Some passengers will have a cabin with a double bed and others will just have berths. Something to think about before setting off...;

— the ages of the passengers – people get more tired on a double decker boat than on a single decker boat;

(© Locaboat Plaisance)

Bedroom

— whether or not there will be children;

— whether or not there is a deck terrace – generally equipped with a second steering post – which, weather permitting, can be used as a solarium, summer dining room and living area. Whatever the model, the level of comfort is generally excellent, with one or more bathrooms,

(© Locaboat Plaisance)

At the helm

(© Locaboat Plaisance)

Lounge

Hiring periods

These pricing periods may vary by a few days or up to a week depending on the region and the hire company.
Very low season: October to late April.
Low season: late April to mid-May and mid-September to early October.
High season: late May to mid-July and late August to mid-September.
Very high season: mid-July to late August.

shower(s), toilet, fitted kitchen (stove, microwave oven, fridge), and garden chairs and table for the deck terrace.
Hire always includes fittings, bedding, crockery and cutlery, boat insurance, technical assistance seven days a week and the log book. It does not include fuel (allow €15-30 per day boating) or cleaning at the end of the trip (up to €150).
A number of optional extras* may be added to these supplements*:

- bike hire (around €30 per week);
- parking costs (between €30 and €50 per week);
- single journey supplement (around €100);
- supplement for pets (around €30 per pet).

(*) These rates provided for information purposes are average prices charged in 2008.

(© Locaboat Plaisance)

Two « Pénichettes » owned by « Locaboat ».

(© Locaboat Plaisance)

A few words of advice

As long as you comply with the regulations, complete the half-hour of training provided by the hire company before setting off and apply basic common sense, river and canal navigation with a licence-free boat should not present any difficulties, even for those who have never before taken the helm. Whatever length boat you choose – up to 15m – they are all easy to manoeuvre, they travel slowly (6 to 8 km/h) and in the event of a problem, all hire companies have response staff available 7 days a week.

Locks

For beginners,passing through the first few locks will doubtless be rather laborious. Applying these basic rules will turn the process into a mere formality.

As you approach a lock, if the gates are shut, stay at a distance to avoid the backwash created by the filling or emptying of the chamber*. When the gates open, leave enough room for boats exiting and only enter the chamber on the green light or on the signal given by the lock-keeper. Approach slowly, having prepared the mooring lines and the fenders* in advance. Impacts may occur, so be careful not to leave any pans on the stove.

(© VNF Pascal Lemaitre)

Canal du Midi, Sallèles d'Aude

In the lock, attach two mooring lines to the mooring bollards* with a simple round turn*, one in front and the other behind. Never moor to ladders and never tie* the mooring lines back onto the boat, or you risk hanging the boat or pulling off the cleats when proceeding downstream*.

Do not remain stationary next to the gates to avoid the risk of running aground on the lock floor*.

When the boat is being raised or lowered, keep the mooring lines taut, loosening or taking in the slack* to avoid the boat turning sideways or colliding with other boats in the chamber at the same time.

Never try to manoeuvre using the engine when in the chamber.

Watch out for ladders and slippery staircases.

When exiting, only release the mooring lines at the end of the lockage cycle, and exit slowly.

Finally, in non-automated locks it is customary for at least one crew member to give the lock-keeper a hand. This does not rule out a well-deserved tip, even if there is no charge for using the locks.

(© VNF Pierre Cheuva)

Canal des Houillères

When navigating

Do not exceed the speed limit of 8km/h, as the wash* may erode the embankments.

Do not travel too close to the embankments; slow down and move back to the middle of the waterway when drawing level with fishermen.

(© VNF Pascal Lemaitre)

The Loire, Montjean

As on the road, keep to the right when passing another boat. Boats proceeding downstream have priority over boats proceeding upstream*. Overtaking* is carried out on the left, and the vessel which is overtaken must slow down to make it easier for the overtaking vessel.

Give way to goods boats and passenger boats.

Turn the vessel's lights on at night or in foggy weather.

When stopping at harbours with facilities, don't forget to stock up on water; however, the fuel reserve is largely sufficient for a week's cruise.

Mooring

With the exception of some very busy harbours, where a small contribution is requested, mooring is free everywhere. You can stop in open country as long as you don't use a private wharf.

Mooring lines must not be tied* to trees or signposts and must not cross the towpath*.

Further information...

It is recommended that children always wear a life jacket and that they do not take part in the locking manoeuvres.

Swimming is not authorised in canals. In navigable rivers it is only authorised in strictly defined areas.

Fishing is authorised in most regions under certain conditions. Make enquiries before setting off and obtain a permit issued by the local authorities.

(*) See "Vocabulary for the freshwater sailor" below.

(© VNF Pascal Lemaitre)

Lutzelbourg Lock, Marne-Rhine Canal

Waterway signs and marking

Mandatory signs

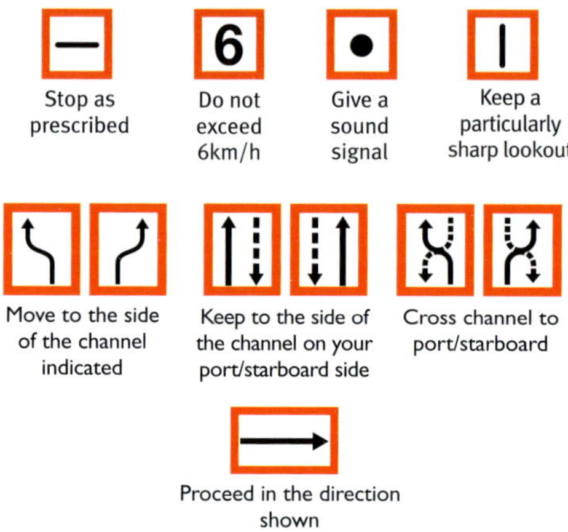

Prohibitory signs

Restrictive signs

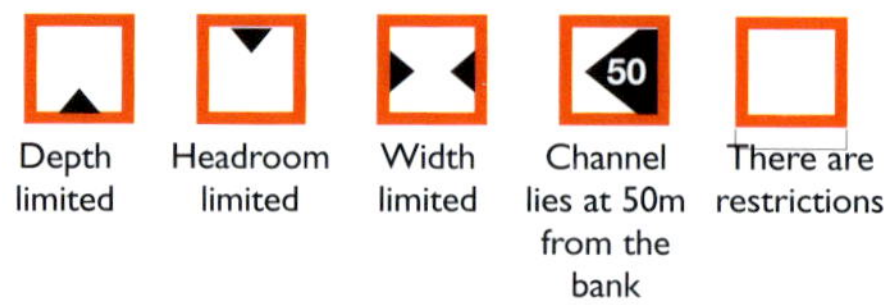

Informative signs

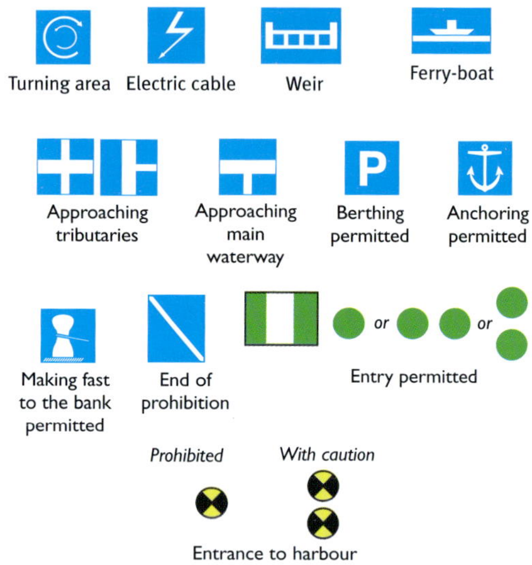

Bridges

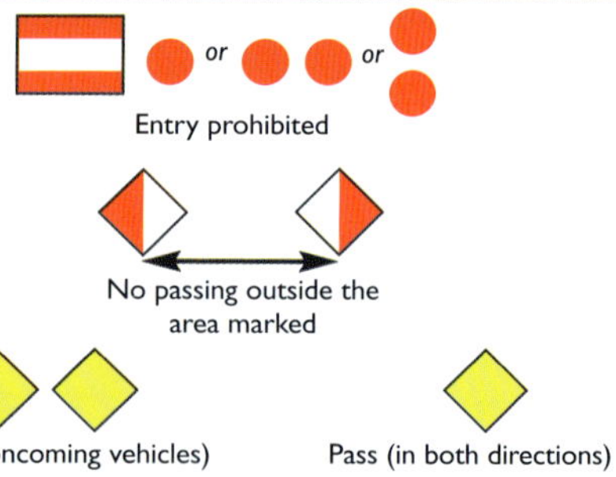

Recommendatory signs

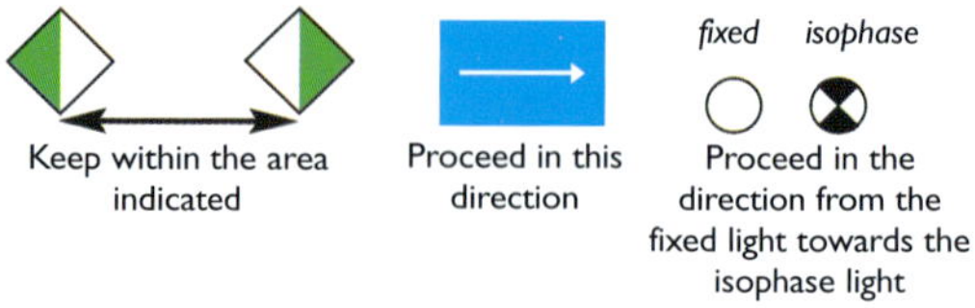

Waterway signs and marking

Marking

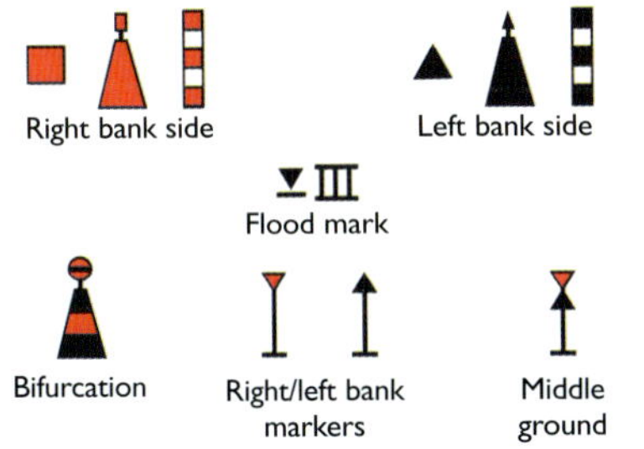

Boats

by night *by day*

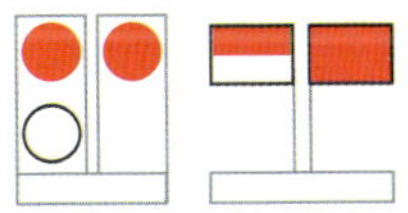

Pass on the side of the red and white lights or boards

Sound signals

Long ■ Short ● Very short • Three-tone ▟

Caution	■
I am altering my course to starboard	●
I am altering my course to port	●●
I am going astern	●●●
I am unable to manoeuvre	●●●●
I cannot be overtaken	●●●●●
Imminent danger of collision	•••••••••• etc.
Distress signal	■■■■ etc.
I am going to turn to starboard	■●
I am going to turn to port	■●●
I wish to overtake on your starboard side	■■●
I wish to overtake on your port side	■■●●
I am going to cross	■■■
Entering and leaving harbours on the starboard side	■■■●
Entering and leaving harbours on the port side	■■■●●
Overcast conditions	
Vessel proceeding alone	■
Convoy or side-by-side formation under way	■■
Vessel proceeding downstream and navigating by radar	▟ ▟ ▟

Key

- Permanent mooring rings
- Mooring rings
- Harbour master's office
- Fuel
- Washroom facilities
- Electricity on quay
- Water on quay
- Public telephone
- Bin
- Shops nearby
- Repairs service
- Launching
- Winter storage
- Car park
- Engine repairs
- Hull repairs
- Sale of fittings
- Sale of engines
- Sale of boats
- Shipyards
- Provisions
- Stop (Right, Left)
- Ramp (Right, Left)
- Lock, Seine basin

The signs and markings of the waterway navigation code are similar to road markings. However, the shapes of the signs are different to avoid confusion when waterways run alongside roads.

Vocabulary for the freshwater sailor

Glossary established using VNF documents.

Air draught
Vertical distance between the level of the waterway and the highest fixed part of the boat, and therefore the clearance under a bridge or tunnel.

(© CRT Midi Pyrénées – Dominique Viet)

Canal du Midi.

Alternating traffic
Alternating one-way system for a narrow passage in which it 0is impossible for two boats to pass.

Aqueduct
A structure to pass a river under a canal or to bring water into the chamber of a lock.

Backlog
Series of boats waiting to enter a lock.

(France-Passion-Plaisance)

Arriving at a lock.

Barge
In the true sense of the word, a barge is a traditional craft which was widespread until the mid-20th century and, at its peak, made up half the French fleet. Its dimensions mean that it can be driven on the Freycinet waterway network.

Bed
The bottom of the canal, between the bases of the slopes which form the embankments.

Berm
The horizontal raised part of the banks bordering a canal.

Bollard
Vertical post made of stone, cast iron or steel for mooring boats at a harbour or a lock.

Canal aqueduct
Structure that enables a canal to cross a river or a narrow valley.

Canal des Deux Mers
Series of waterways comprising the Canal du Midi, the Canal de Brienne, the Canal de Jonction, the Canal de la Robine and the Canal Latéral à la Garonne.

Canal du Midi
Waterway between Toulouse and Lagoon of Thau.

Cast anchor
Lower the anchor into the water.

Chamber
The part of the lock between its two gates.

Change course
When a boat changes direction, this is known as changing course. Turning areas, sometimes

known as winding holes, are provided to enable boats to change course.

Chartering
Hiring out of a tourist boat.

Check
Manoeuvre to gradually bring a boat to a standstill, holding it back with a mooring line attached to the boat and to a mooring bollard on the quay.

Come alongside
Draw up next to a quay or parallel with another vessel.

Coupling
Attaching two boats side by side.

Cruiser
Pleasure boat less than 15 metres long.

Depth of navigable channel
Depth available for a boat to pass.

Dolphin
Pile allowing a boat to be moored in a reach near a lock.

Downstream
Part of the canal between a particular point and the canal junction.

Draught
Height of the part of the vessel that is under water. The draught therefore varies depending on the load. The word is sometimes wrongly used to mean depth of navigable channel, which refers to the depth of the canal. Between the depth of navigable channel and the draught, a minimum depth (20 to 50cm), known as the safety margin, must be respected.

Driven off course
Describes a boat pushed into the path of a hazard by the wind or the current.

Drop astern
Drift backwards with the current.

Drop wall
A sort of step, located immediately downstream of the upstream lock gate, which spans the difference in level between the upstream and downstream reaches.

Embankment
Bank running alongside a canal.

Fender
A sort of flexible cushioning device to protect the hull against impacts or abrasion.

Floating bollard
Mooring device that rises or falls in the lock at the same time as the boat.

Freycinet
Charles-Louis de Saulces de Freycinet, French Minister for Public Works from 1877 to 1879, established standards for a number of transport regulations. His name was given to a gauge which is applied to boats and canals. A "Freycinet" barge is 38.5m long and 5.05m wide. A "Freycinet" lock is 39m long and 5.2m wide.

Gangplank
Plank used to bridge the gap between a vessel and the embankment.

Gauge
The gauge of a waterway indicates the size of the largest boats that can use it, in terms of length, width, draught and air draught.

(© Y. Martin)

The towpath, Nantes-Brest Canal

Towpaths

Whether navigating or walking along towpaths, it should never be forgotten that they are above all used for waterway maintenance. Article 62 of the 1932 French decree stipulates that towpaths are only available for use on foot. Any breach of this rule will be subject to a 'contravention de grande voirie', a fine which may be as high as €12,000. The French waterways authority (Voies Navigables de France – VNF) has, however, concluded agreements with local authorities to promote the establishment of 'green ways', which follow the routes of towpaths. Bikes, and sometimes horses, are now authorised to use this ever-increasing network of specially developed trails. Motor vehicles, however, even those with two wheels, are strictly prohibited. Be careful – never enter a prohibited section, even on foot, as collapsing embankments can represent a real danger. Cyclists and horse-riders must dismount as they approach fishermen. Despite these very modest restrictions, towpaths can provide wonderful opportunities for walking and offer a genuine alternative to boating.

(© CRT Midi Pyrénées – Dominique Viet)

A « voie verte » pathway on the Canal du Midi.

Gear
All the equipment and fittings necessary for operating a boat.

Kilometre point
Kilometre point, indicated by a marker and included on all canal maps. This is essential for helping you locate your position in relation to a lock, a bridge or a location.

Lighter
Flat-bottomed boat with no deck, used for transporting goods.

Lockage
All the manoeuvres required for a boat to pass through a lock.

Lock floor
Slab forming the base of a lock chamber.

Lock wall
Lateral wall of a lock.

Make a U-turn
Change course through 180°.

Overtake
Draw even with and move past another boat. Overtaking is often prohibited near engineering structures.

Port side
What is to the left of the boat when looking forwards.

Proceeding downstream
Describes a boat which travels down the current or heads downstream on a canal with a summit reach.

(© CRT Midi Pyrénées – Dominique Viet)

Canal du Midi.

Proceeding upstream
Describes a boat which travels against the current or heads upstream on a canal with a summit reach.

Reach
Portion of a canal between two locks.

Revetment
Any system of protection for the embankments of a canal, consisting of lines of piles supporting an intermediate material, fascines, wood, metal or concrete.

Round turn
A simple turn made with a mooring line around a cleat or a mooring bollard to enable the tension of the line to be controlled.

Saloon
"Living room" on a boat.

Sluice gate
The moving part of a lock gate.

Span
The width of a stretch of water between the two embankments.

Spillway
Structure with manoeuvrable sluices that allow the excess water in a canal to be run off from the base.

Starboard
What is to the right of the boat when looking forwards.

Stoppage
Period during which navigation is interrupted for canal maintenance works.

Tackle
Anything relating to a boat's rigging equipment.

Take in the slack
Tighten a mooring line by bringing it on board, in order to draw alongside a quay, for example.

Tie
Attach a mooring line to a cleat on the boat or to a mooring bollard on the quay.

(©VNF Pascal Lemaitre)

Canal de la Robine.

Towpath
Towpaths were once used by people and horses to tow boats. Today they are used for the maintenance and operation of canals and rivers. Unless otherwise indicated, they can be used by walkers. 'Opposite towpath' refers to the towpath situated on the opposite bank.

Upstream
Part of the canal between a particular point and the summit reach.

Victual
Load a boat with the provisions required for the daily life of the crew and the operation of the boat.

Wash
The wake of a boat.

Weir
Structure enabling the excess water of a reach to be run off by spilling over the top, without human intervention. Not to be confused with spillway (see above).

Useful addresses

A) The government-funded French waterways authority (Voies Navigables de France – VNF)

The French waterways authority (Voies Navigables de France - VNF) is responsible for the management, operation, modernisation and development of Europe's largest waterway network, which comprises 6,700km of canals and rivers, over 2,000 engineering structures and 40,000 hectares of public land. It is a government-funded public undertaking under the authority of the Ministry of Ecology, Energy, Sustainable Development and Land Use Planning, and works closely with institutions and waterway users. It is involved in all the policies associated with the preservation and sustainable development of the waterways.

Headquarters

VNF - 175 rue Ludovic-Boutleux
BP 820, 62408 Béthune
Cedex, France
Tel.: +33 (0)3 21 63 24 24.
Fax: +33 (0)3 21 63 24 42

(© Locaboat Holidays)

Local directorates

Direction régionale
du Nord-Pas-de-Calais
Service de la navigation
du Nord-Pas-de-Calais
37 rue du Plat,
59034 Lille Cedex,
France
Tel.: +33 (0)3 20 15 49 70.
Fax: +33 (0)3 20 15 49 71
Email: SN-Nord-Pas-de-Calais@equipement.gouv.fr
Website: www.equipement.gouv.fr/sn-npc

Direction interrégionale
du Bassin de la Seine
Service de la navigation
de la Seine 2 quai de Grenelle,
75732 Paris Cedex 15,
France
Tel.: +33 (0)1 40 58 29 99.
Fax: +33 (0)1 45 78 08 57
Email: SN-seine@equipement.gouv.fr
Website: http://www.sn-seine.equipement.gouv.fr/

Direction interrégionale
du Nord-Est Service
de la navigation du Nord-Est
28 boulevard Albert-Ier, CO 62,
54036 Nancy Cedex, France
Tel.: +33 (0)3 83 95 30 01.
Fax: +33 (0)3 83 98 56 61
Email: SN-Nord-Est@equipement.gouv.fr

(© France-Passion-Plaisance)

Direction interrégionale
de Strasbourg Service
de la navigation de Strasbourg
25 rue de la Nuée-Bleue,
BP 30367, 67010 Strasbourg
Cedex, France
Tel.: +33 (0)3 88 21 74 74.
Fax: +33 (0)3 88 75 65 06
Email: SN-Strasbourg@equipement.gouv.fr

Direction interrégionale
du Centre-Est DDE
de la Nièvre
2 rue de Pâtis, BP 69,
58020 Nevers Cedex, France
Tel.: +33 (0)3 86 71 71 71.
Fax: +33 (0)3 86 61 28 96
Email: DDE-Nievre@equipement.gouv.fr

Direction interrégionale
du Rhône-Saône Service
de la navigation Rhône-Saône
2 rue de la Quarantaine,
69321 Lyon Cedex 05, France
Tel.: +33 (0)4 72 56 59 00.
Fax: +33 (0)4 72 56 59 01
Email: SN-Rhone-Saone@equipement.gouv.fr

Direction interrégionale
du Sud-Ouest Service
de la navigation du Sud-Ouest
2 Port Saint-Étienne, BP 7204,
31073 Toulouse Cedex 7, France
Tel.: +33 (0)5 61 36 24 24.
Fax: +33 (0)5 61 54 66 50
Email: SN-Toulouse@equipement.gouv.fr

B) Where to hire a licence-free boat

There are around a hundred rental stations across the French waterway network offering over 2,000 boats of all sizes and models. We are unable to provide details here of all the local hire companies. The companies whose addresses are listed below can be found throughout France.

CONNOISSEUR

Le Grand Bassin,
BP 1201, 11492 Castelnaudary,
France
Tel.: +33 (0)4 68 94 09 75.
Fax: +33 (0)4 68 94 52 73
Email: info@connoisseur.fr
Website: www.connoisseur.fr

FRANCE-PASSION-PLAISANCE

Maison du Bateau,
Port de Plaisance,
71160 Digoin, France
Tel.: +33 (0)3 85 53 76 70.
Fax: +33 (0)3 85 53 76 71
Email: contact@france-passion-plaisance.fr
Website: www.france-passion-plaisance.fr

RIVE DE FRANCE

Port de Plaisance,
34440 Colombiers, France
Tel.: 0810 80 80 80
(France only).
Fax: +33 (0)4 67 37 60 03
Email: rdf@rivedefrance.com
Website: www.rive-de-france.com

CROWN BLUE LINE

Le Grand Bassin, BP 1201,
Castelnaudary Cedex, France
Tel.: +33 (0)4 68 94 52 72.
Fax: +33 (0)4 68 94 52 73
Email: info@crownblueline.com
Website: www.crownblueline.fr

NICOLS

Route du Puy-Saint-Bonnet,
49300 Cholet, France
Tel.: +33 (0)2 41 56 46 56
Email: nicols@nicols.com
Website: www.nicols.com

(© Locaboat Holidays)

LOCABOAT HOLIDAYS

BP 150,
89303 Joigny Cedex, France
Tel.: +33 (0)3 86 91 72 72
Email: info@locaboat.com
Website: www.locaboat.com

(© Locaboat Holidays)

Bibliography

GENERAL WORKS

Canaux de France, Michel-Paul Simon, Ed. du Chêne, 1999.

Les Canaux de France, André Papazian, Ed. Ouest-France, 2009.

Histoire des canaux, fleuves et rivières de France, Pierre Micquel, Ed. No. 1, 1994.

Guides fluviaux, Ed. du Breil.

Cinq siècles de transport fluvial en France : XVIIe-XIXe, Laurent Roblin, Ed. Ouest-France, 2003.

Canaux, rivières des hommes, Pierre Pinon, Ed. Rempart-Desclée de Brouwer, 1995.

Mariniers, Bernard Le Sueur, Le Chasse-Marée, 2004.

(© Locaboat Holidays)

Le Tourisme fluvial, Marie-Madeleine Damien, PUF, collection « Que sais-je ? », 2001.

Le Transport fluvial en France, Alain Boussuge, ONN, 1990.

Canaux, fleuves et rivières de France, André Papazian and Michel Destombes, Ed. Massin, 2005.

Batelleries et batelliers (sic) *de France : Histoire illustrée de la navigation intérieure*, Bernard Le Sueur and François Beaudouin, Ed. Horvath, 1985.

SPECIALIST WORKS

Le Canal du Midi, histoire d'un chef-d'œuvre, René Gast and Bruno Barbier, Ed. Ouest-France, 2006.

Le Canal des Deux-Mers, André Maistre, Ed. Privat, 1968.

Connaissance du Canal du Midi, Arnaud d'Antin de Vaillac, Ed. France-Empire, 1997.

Le Canal du Midi, Francis Loubatières, Ed. Loubatières, 1997.

Le Canal du Midi, Jean-Denis Bergasse and Michel Adgé, Ed. Tallandier, 1989.

Le Canal du Midi et le canal latéral à la Garonne, Louis Destrem, Ed. du Chêne, 1996.

Le Canal du Midi et les voies navigables de l'Atlantique à la Méditerranée, René Gast, photos Jacques Debru, Ed. Ouest-France, 2009.

Un canal, des canaux, catalogue of the exhibition held in Paris from 7 March to 8 June 1986 in the Conciergerie, published by the Caisse nationale des monuments historiques et des sites, 1986.

Une histoire de la marine de Loire, Patrick Villiers and Annick Senotier, Ed. Grandvaux, 1997.

Le Canal de Bourgogne, Christine Baron Languet, Ed. de l'Armançon, 1994.

Au fil du canal de Bourgogne, Ed. Hachette, 2002.

Le Canal de l'Ourcq, Vie et anecdotes, Michel Mérille, Amarco Editions, 1996.

Les Canaux de l'Ourcq, Jacques de la Garde, Sauvegarde des monuments, 1991.

Les Canaux de Paris,
Collective work, Mairie de Paris/DGIC, 1998.

Les Canaux de Paris, Collective work, "Paris et son patrimoine" collection, Délégation à l'action artistique et culturelle de la Ville de Paris, Distributed by the CNRS, 1994.

Les Canaux parisiens,
Marc Gayda, Ed. de l'Ormet, 1995.

Je me souviens du canal Saint-Martin, Marie Babey, Ed. Parigramme, 1996.

Balades au bord de l'eau en Ile-de-France,
Jean-Pierre Hervet and Patrick Mérienne, Ed. Ouest-France, 1998.

Entre Isle et Rance : un canal, des hommes, des femmes,
Ed. Danclau, 1993.

En passant par la Vilaine, de Redon à Rennes en 1543, Ed. Apogée, 1997.

La Batellerie bretonne,
J. Guillet, J.-P. Cébron, E. Guyomard, Le Chasse-Marée-Ed. de l'Estran, 1988.

L'Escaut sans frontière,
M. Voiturier, P. Meire, J. Decreton, La Renaissance du Livre, 2000.

Le Canal de Nantes à Brest,
Kader Benferhat, Sandra Aubert and Richard Nourry, Ed. Ouest-France, 1999.

La Bretagne des canaux,
Kader Benferhat and Hervé Ronné, Ed. Ouest-France, 2006.

Les Canaux du Nord et du Pas-de-Calais,
Ed. Ouest-France, 2006.

Les Canaux de Paris,
Jean-Pierre Hervet and Patrick Mérienne, Geoffroy Deffrenes and Samuel Dhote, Ed. Ouest-France, 2002.

Les Canaux de Bourgogne,
Catherine Parinet and Alain Parinet, Ed. Ouest-France, 2008.

Le Canal du Midi et les voies navigables de l'Atlantique à la Méditerranée,
René Gast and Bruno Barbier, Ed. Ouest-France, 2000.

(© Yves Martin)

Chemins d'eau : les canaux du Centre,
Valérie Mauret-Cribelier and Charles Berg, musée de la Marine de Loire de Châteauneuf-sur-Loire, 2004.

Balades au fil de l'eau : rivières et canaux de France,
Gilles Plazy. Selection from the Reader's Digest, 2002.

L'Aventure intérieure : Des canaux en Bretagne,
Y. Pallier and N. Richard, Ed. Apogée, 1999.

Canaux et batellerie en Alsace : Histoire et anecdotes,
René Descombes, Ed. Le Verger, 1988.

Index of place names

The page numbers appearing in bold refer to the images.

Table of contents

Editor: Anne Cauquetoux
Editorial Coordination: Isabelle Rousseau
Graphics design and Page layout: Graphics Studio at Éditions Ouest-France
Cartography: Patrick Mérienne
Photoengraving: Scann'Ouest, Rennes (35)
Printing: Imprimerie Pollina at Luçon (85) - L60638B

Édilarge SA, Rennes
ISBN 978-2-7373-4671-2
Editor No. 5850.02.01.05.12
Copyright: January 2009
Printed in France
Visit us at www.editionsouestfrance.fr